Bhimrao Ramji Ambedkar (1891–1956) is one of India's most radical thinkers. He transformed the social and political landscape in the struggle against British colonialism. He was a prolific writer who oversaw the drafting of the Indian Constitution and served as India's first Law Minister. In 1935, he publicly declared "I had the misfortune of being born with the 'Untouchable Hindu' stain ... [but] I will not die as a person who calls himself a Hindu!" Ambedkar eventually embraced Buddhism, a few months before his death in 1956.

*Every day was a b*** steak day*

B.R. Ambedkar

ISBN 9788195838578

Annotated selections from *The Untouchables: Who Were They and Why They Became Untouchables?* published 1948 by Amrit Book Depot, Delhi

Annotated by Alex George and S. Anand

This edition is published in 2024 on the occasion of 20 years of Navayana as part of the EVERBLUE series.

Navayana Publishing Pvt Ltd
155 2nd Floor
Shahpur Jat, New Delhi 110049
navayana.org

Typeset in Dante MT Std by InoSoft Systems, Noida
Printed by Sanjiv Palliwal, New Delhi
Subscribe to updates at navayana.org/subscribe

Distributed in South Asia by HarperCollins India

EVERY DAY WAS A B*** STEAK DAY

Annotated Selections from *The Untouchables: Who Were They and Why They Became Untouchables?*

B.R. AMBEDKAR

edited and annotated by
Alex George and S. Anand

[Ambedkar's dedication, 1948]

Inscribed to the memory of

NANDNAR

RAVIDAS

CHOKHAMELA

THREE RENOWNED SAINTS WHO WERE BORN AMONG THE UNTOUCHABLES AND WHO BY THEIR PIETY AND VIRTUE WON THE ESTEEM OF ALL

Contents

A note on this selection

B.R. Ambedkar's *The Untouchables: Who Were They and Why They Became Untouchables?*—the sequel to his 1946 work, *The Shudras: Who they were and How they came to be the Fourth Varna of the Indo-Aryan Society*—was first published in October 1948 by Amrit Book Co., Delhi. It is an investigation into the origins of Untouchability, self-declared as 'a pioneer attempt in the exploration of a field so completely neglected by everybody'. The long history of Brahmanism, and the persistence of its colonizing efforts and effects, are predicated on the naturalisation of caste and Untouchability. Harking back to the Buddhist tradition of anti-metaphysical thinking—that asserted the this-worldliness and materiality of all perceivable phenomena—Ambedkar refutes these pretensions. Not content with the mere naming of Untouchability as immoral, Ambedkar begins from the premise that its very existence is 'most unnatural'.

This selection was first published by Navayana (and simultaneously published by Columbia University Press) in 2019 as *Beef, Brahmins and Broken Men: An Annotated Critical Selection from* 'The Untouchables'. It came at a time when cow-vigilantism was on the rise and the rhetoric of cow-protectionism had resulted in atrocities against scores of Muslims and Dalits. Given the situation, we turned to Ambedkar, who in this classic text revealed the vacuity of any claims of primordial Hindu 'bovinophilia'. The original text was dense with references to ancient and medieval literature from the Brahmanic as well as the Buddhist canon. As editors, we saw to it that all these threads were detangled and all avenues of speculative connections to contemporary academic developments were explored. The result was a book that was close to four hundred pages long, with copious annotations, and an extensive introduction by the renowned intellectual Kancha Ilaiah Shepherd. It was a valuable resource to scholars and students alike.

The attempt now is to bring the heft of Ambedkar's scholarship to the general reader. We have reduced and shortened the many annotations. Ambedkar's footnotes have been left intact; they appear in square brackets alongside the annotations. In the following pages, you will discover how Vedic Brahmanism was built on the sacrifice of the cow, and how Buddhism emerged to put a spanner in the works. Brahmanism foiled the hegemony of this new doctrine of temperance by appropriating its tenets and taking it to a new extreme.

Ambedkar's history is often speculative and imaginative. In his time, there was little interest in academia to answer the question that became the subtitle of his 1948 book: *Who were the Untouchables and how did they become Untouchable?* Unfortunately, not much has changed since. Indian history is overrun with mythological and religious ideologies, which further obscure objective truths of our collective violent past. Ambedkar answers this challenge by looking for the most feasible and rational answers based on the available evidence. He anticipates criticisms that could, and have been, raised against him for breaching disciplinary and caste lines, and taking ancient religious texts to task, and treating them as sociological testimonies of violence:

> It may well turn out that this attempt of mine is only an illustration of the proverbial fool rushing in where the angels dare not tread. But I take refuge in the belief that even the

> fool has a duty to perform, namely, to do his bit if the angel has gone to sleep or is unwilling to proclaim the truth. (1990b: 11).

Let us join him on this journey to where angels dare not go. Our terminus is the truth, not the comfort of inaction.

Alex George & S. Anand

1 April 2024

Preface

This book is a sequel to my treatise called *The Shudras—Who they were and How they came to be the Fourth Varna of the Indo-Aryan Society*[1] which was published in 1946. Besides the Shudras, the Hindu Civilization has produced three social classes whose existence has not received the attention it deserves. The three classes are:

i. The Criminal Tribes[2] who number about 20 million or so;
ii. The Aboriginal Tribes[3] who number about 15 million; and
iii. The Untouchables who number about 50 million.

The existence of these classes is an abomination. The Hindu Civilization, gauged in the light of these social products, could hardly be called civilization. It is a diabolical contrivance to suppress and enslave humanity. Its proper name would be infamy. What else can be said of a civilization which has produced a mass of people who are taught to accept crime as an approved means of earning their livelihood, another mass of people who are left to live in full bloom of their primitive barbarism in the midst of civilization and a third mass of people who are treated as an entity beyond human intercourse and whose mere touch is enough to cause pollution?

In any other country the existence of these classes would have led to searching of the heart and to investigation of their origin. But neither of these has occurred to the mind of the Hindu. The reason is simple. The Hindu does not regard the existence of these classes as a matter of apology or shame and feels no responsibility either to atone for it or to inquire into its origin and growth. On the other hand, every Hindu is taught to believe that his civilization is not only the most ancient but that it is also in many respects altogether unique. No Hindu ever feels tired of repeating these claims. That the Hindu Civilization is the most ancient, one can understand and even allow. But it is not quite so easy to understand on what grounds they rely for claiming that the Hindu Civilization is a unique one. The Hindus may not like it, but so far as it strikes non-Hindus, such a claim can rest only on one ground. It is the existence of these classes for which the Hindu Civilization is responsible. That the existence of such classes is a unique phenomenon, no Hindu need repeat, for nobody can deny the fact. One only wishes that the Hindu realized that it was a matter for which there was more cause for shame than pride.

The inculcation of these false beliefs in the sanity, superiority and sanctity of Hindu Civilization is due entirely to the peculiar social psychology of Hindu scholars.

To-day all scholarship is confined to the Brahmins. But unfortunately no Brahmin scholar has so far come forward to play the part of a Voltaire[4] who had the intellectual honesty to rise against the doctrines of the Catholic Church in which he was brought up; nor is one likely to appear on the scene in the future. It is a grave reflection on the scholarship of the Brahmins that they should not have produced a Voltaire. This will not cause surprise if it is remembered that the Brahmin scholar is only a learned man. He is not an intellectual. There is a world of difference between one who is learned and one who is an intellectual. The former is class-conscious and is alive to the interests of his class. The latter is an emancipated being who is free to act without being swayed by class considerations. It is because the Brahmins have been only learned men that they have not produced a Voltaire.

Why have the Brahmins not produced a Voltaire? The question can be answered only by another question. Why did the Sultan of Turkey not abolish the religion of the Mohammedan World? Why has no Pope denounced Catholicism? Why has the British Parliament not made a law ordering the killing of all blue-eyed babies? The reason why the Sultan or the Pope or the British Parliament has not done these things is the same as why the Brahmins have not been able to produce a Voltaire. It must be recognized that the selfish interest of a person or of the class to which he belongs always acts as an internal limitation which regulates the direction of his intellect. The power and position which the Brahmins possess is entirely due to the Hindu Civilization which treats them as supermen and subjects the lower classes to all sorts of disabilities so that they may never rise and challenge or threaten the superiority of the Brahmins over them. As is natural, every Brahmin is interested in the maintenance of Brahmanic supremacy be he orthodox or unorthodox, be he a priest or a grahastha, be he a scholar or not. How can the Brahmins afford to be Voltaires? A Voltaire among the Brahmins would be a positive danger to the maintenance of a civilization which is contrived to maintain Brahmanic supremacy. The point is that the intellect of a Brahmin scholar is severely limited by anxiety to preserve his interest. He suffers from this internal limitation as a result of which he does not allow his intellect full play which honesty and integrity demands. For, he fears that it may affect the interests of his class and therefore his own.

But what annoys one is the intolerance of the Brahmin scholar towards any attempt to expose the Brahmanic literature. He himself would not play the part of an iconoclast even where it is necessary. And he would not allow such non-Brahmins as have the capacity to do so to play it. If any non-Brahmin were to make such an attempt the Brahmin scholars would engage in a conspiracy of silence, take no notice of him, condemn him outright on some flimsy grounds or dub his work useless. As a writer engaged in the exposition of the Brahmanic literature I have been a victim of such mean tricks.

Notwithstanding the attitude of the Brahmin scholars, I must pursue the task I have undertaken. For the origin of these classes is a subject which still awaits investigation. This book deals with one of these unfortunate classes namely, the Untouchables. The Untouchables are the most numerous of the three. Their existence is also the most unnatural. And yet there has so far been no investigation into their origin. That the Hindus should not have undertaken such an investigation is perfectly understandable. The old orthodox Hindu does not think that there is anything wrong in the observance of Untouchability. To him it is a normal and natural thing. As such it neither calls for expiation nor explanation. The new modern Hindu realizes the wrong. But he is ashamed to discuss it in public for fear of letting the foreigner know that Hindu Civilization can be guilty of such a vicious and infamous system or social code as evidenced by Untouchability. But what is strange is that Untouchability should have failed to attract the attention of the European student of social institutions. It is difficult to understand why. The fact, however, is there.

This book may, therefore, be taken as a pioneer attempt in the exploration of a field so completely neglected by everybody. The book, if I may say so, deals not only with every aspect of the main question set out for inquiry, namely, the origin of Untouchability, but it also deals with almost all questions connected with it. Some of the questions are such that very few people are even aware of them; and those who are aware of them are puzzled by them and do not know how to answer them. To mention only a few, the book deals with such questions as: Why do the Untouchables live outside the village? Why did beef-eating give rise to Untouchability? Did the Hindus never eat beef? Why did non-Brahmins give up beef-eating? What made the Brahmins become vegetarians, etc.? To each one of these, the book suggests an answer. It may be that the answers given in the book to these questions are not all-embracing. Nonetheless it will be found that the book points to a new way of looking at old things.

The thesis on the origin of Untouchability advanced in the book is an altogether novel thesis. It comprises the following propositions:

1. There is no racial difference between the Hindus and the Untouchables;
2. The distinction between the Hindus and Untouchables in its original form, before the advent of Untouchability, was the distinction between Tribesmen and Broken Men from alien Tribes. It is the Broken Men who subsequently came to be treated as Untouchables;
3. Just as Untouchability has no racial basis so also has it no occupational basis;
4. There are two roots from which Untouchability has sprung:
    i. Contempt and hatred of the Broken Men as of Buddhists by the Brahmins:
    ii. Continuation of beef-eating by the Broken Men after it had been given up by others.
5. In searching for the origin of Untouchability care must be taken to distinguish the Untouchables from the Impure. All orthodox Hindu writers have identified the Impure with the Untouchables. This is an error. Untouchables are distinct from the Impure.
6. While the Impure as a class came into existence at the time of

the Dharma Sutras the Untouchables came into being much later than 400 AD.

These conclusions are the result of such historical research as I have been able to make. The ideal which a historian should place before himself has been well defined by Goethe[5] who said:[6]

> [453] The historian's duty is to separate the true from the false, the certain from the uncertain, and the doubtful from that which cannot be accepted. ... [543] Every investigator must before all things look upon himself as one who is summoned to serve on a jury. He has only to consider how far the statement of the case is complete and clearly set forth by the evidence. Then he draws his conclusion and gives his vote, whether it be that his opinion coincides with that of the foreman or not.

There can be no difficulty in giving effect to Goethe's direction when the relevant and necessary facts are forthcoming. All this advice is of course very valuable and very necessary. But Goethe does not tell what the historian is to do when he comes across a missing link, when no direct evidence of connected relations between important events is available. I mention this because in the course of my investigations into the origin of Untouchability and other interconnected problems I have been confronted with many missing links. It is true that I am not the only one who has been confronted with them. All students of ancient Indian history have had to face them. For as Mountstuart Elphinstone[7] has observed in Indian history 'no date of a public event can be fixed before the invasion of Alexander; and no *connected* relation of the natural transactions can be attempted until after the Mohametan conquest.'[8] This is a sad confession but that again does not help. The question is: 'What is a student of history to do? Is he to cry halt and stop his work until the link is discovered?' I think not. I believe that in such cases it is permissible for him to use his imagination and intuition to bridge the gaps left in the chain of facts by links not yet discovered and to propound a working hypothesis suggesting how facts which cannot be connected by known facts might have been inter-connected. I must admit that rather than hold up the work, I have preferred to resort to this means to get over the difficulty created by the missing links which have come in my way.

Critics may use this weakness to condemn the thesis as violating the canons of historical research. If such be the attitude of the critics I must remind them that if there is a law which governs the evaluation of the results of historical results then refusal to accept a thesis on the ground that it is based on direct evidence is bad law. Instead of concentrating themselves on the issue of direct evidence versus inferential evidence and inferential evidence versus speculation, what the critics should concern themselves with is to examine (i) whether the thesis is based on pure conjecture, and (ii) whether the thesis is possible and if so does it fit in with facts better than mine does?

On the first issue I could say that the thesis would not be unsound merely because in some parts it is based on guesswork. My critics should remember that we are dealing with an institution the origin of which is lost to antiquity. The present attempt to explain the origin of Untouchability is not the same as writing history from texts which speak with certainty. It is a case of reconstructing history where there are no texts, and if there are, they have no direct bearing on the question. In such circumstances what one has to do is to strive to divine what the texts conceal or suggest without being even quite certain of having found the truth. The task is one of gathering survivals of the past, placing them together and making them tell the story of their birth. The task is analogous to that of the archaeologist who constructs a city from broken stones or of the palaeontologist who conceives an extinct animal from scattered bones and teeth or of a painter who reads the lines of the horizon and the smallest vestiges on the slopes of the hill to make up a scene. In this sense the book is a work of art even more than of history.

The origin of Untouchability lies buried in a dead past which nobody knows. To make it alive is like an attempt to reclaim to history a city which has been dead since ages past and present it as it was in its original condition. It cannot but be that imagination and hypothesis should play a large part in such a work. But that in itself cannot be a ground for the condemnation of the thesis. For without trained imagination no scientific inquiry can be fruitful and hypothesis is the very soul of science. As Maxim Gorky[9] has said:[10]

> Science and literature have much in common; in both, observation, comparison and study are of fundamental importance; the artist like the scientist, needs both imagination and intuition. Imagination and intuition bridge the gaps in the chain of facts by its as yet undiscovered links and permit the scientist to create hypothesis and theories which more or less correctly and successfully direct the searching of the mind in its study of the forms and phenomenon of nature. They are of literary creation; the art of creating characters and types demands imagination, intuition, the ability to make things up in one's own mind.

It is therefore unnecessary for me to apologize for having resorted to constructing links where they were missing. Nor can my thesis be said to be vitiated on that account for nowhere is the construction of links based on pure conjecture. The thesis in great part is based on facts and inferences from facts. And where it is not based on facts or inferences from facts, it is based on circumstantial evidence of presumptive character resting on considerable degree of probability. There is nothing that I have urged in support of my thesis which I have asked my readers to accept on trust. I have at least shown that there exists a preponderance of probability in favour of what I have asserted. It would be nothing but pedantry to say that a preponderance of probability is not a sufficient basis for a valid decision.

On the second point with the examination of which, I said, my critics should concern themselves what I would like to say is that I am not so vain as to claim any finality for my thesis. I do not ask them to accept it as the last word. I do not wish to influence their judgement. They are of course free to come to their own conclusion. All I say to them is to consider whether this thesis is not a workable and therefore, for the time being, a valid hypothesis, if the test of a valid hypothesis is that it should fit in with all surrounding facts, explain them and give them a meaning which in its absence they do not appear to have. I do not want anything more from my critics than a fair and unbiased appraisal.

B.R. Ambedkar
January 1, 1948
1, Hardinge Avenue,
New Delhi.

Part IV

NEW THEORIES OF THE ORIGIN OF UNTOUCHABILITY

Chapter IX
Contempt for Buddhists as the root of Untouchability

I

THE Census Reports for India published by the Census Commissioner at the interval of every ten years from 1870 onwards contain a wealth of information nowhere else to be found regarding the social and religious life of the people of India. Before the Census of 1910 the Census Commissioner had a column called "Population by Religion". Under this heading the population was shown (1) Muslims, (2) Hindus, (3) Christians, etc. The Census Report for the year 1910 marked a new departure from the prevailing practice. For the first time it divided the Hindus under three separate categories, (i) Hindus, (ii) Animists and Tribal,[1] and (iii) the Depressed Classes or Untouchables. This new classification has been continued ever since.

II

This departure from the practice of the previous Census Commissioners raises three questions.[2] First is, what led the Commissioner for the Census of 1910 to introduce this new classification. The second is what were the criteria adopted as a basis for this classification. The third is what are the reasons for the growth of certain practices which justify the division of Hindus into the three separate categories mentioned above.

The answer to the first question will be found in the address presented in 1909[3] by the Muslim Community under leadership of H.H. The Aga Khan[4] to the then Viceroy, Lord Minto, in which they asked for a separate and adequate representation for the Muslim community in the legislature, executive and the public services. In the address[5] there occurs the following passage:

> The Mohamedans of India number, according to the census taken in the year 1901, over sixty-two millions or between one-fifth and one-fourth of the total population of His Majesty's Indian dominions, *and if a reduction be made for the uncivilized portions of the community enumerated under the heads of animist and other minor religions, as well as for those classes who are ordinarily classified as Hindus but properly speaking are not Hindus at all, the proportion of Mohamedans to the Hindu Majority becomes much larger.*[6] We therefore desire to submit that under any system of representation extended or limited a community in itself more numerous than the entire population of any first class European power except Russia may justly lay claim to adequate recognition as an important factor in the State.
>
> We venture, indeed, with Your Excellency's permission to go a step further, and urge that the position accorded to the Mohamedan community in any kind of representation direct or indirect, and in all other ways effecting their status and influence should be commensurate, not merely with their numerical strength but also with their political importance and the value of the contribution which they make to the defence of the empire, and we also hope that Your Excellency will in this connection be pleased to give due consideration to the position which they occupied in India a little more than hundred years ago and of which the traditions have naturally not faded from their minds.[7]

The portion in italics has a special significance. It was introduced in the address to suggest that in comprising the numerical strength of the Muslims with that of the Hindus the population of the Animists, tribals and the Untouchables should be excluded. The reason for this new classification of 'Hindus' adopted by the Census Commissioner in 1910 lies in this demand of the Muslim community for separate representation on augmented scale. At any rate this is how the Hindus understood this demand.[8]

Interesting as it is, the first question as to why the Census Commissioner made this departure in the system of classification is of less importance than the second question. What is important is to know the basis adopted by the Census Commissioner for separating the different classes of Hindus into (1) those who were hundred per cent Hindus and (2) those who were not.

The basis adopted by the Census Commissioner for separation is to be found in the circular issued by him in which he laid down certain tests for the purpose[9] of distinguishing these two classes. Among those who were not hundred per cent Hindus included castes and tribes which:

1. Deny the supremacy of the Brahmins.
2. Do not receive the mantra from a Brahmin or other recognized Hindu guru.
3. Deny the authority of the Vedas.
4. Do not worship the Hindu gods.
5. Are not served by good Brahmins as family priests.
6. Have no Brahmin priests at all.
7. Are denied access to the interior of the Hindu temples.
8. Cause pollution (a) by touch, or (b) within a certain distance.
9. Bury their dead.
10. Eat beef and do no reverence to the cow.

Out of these ten tests some divide the Hindus from the Animists and the Tribal.[10] The rest divide the Hindus from the Untouchables. Those that divide the Untouchables from the Hindus are (2), (5), (6), (7), and (10). It is with them that we are chiefly concerned.[11]

For the sake of clarity it is better to divide these tests into parts and consider them separately. This chapter will be devoted only to the consideration of (2), (5), and (6).

The replies received by the Census Commissioner to questions embodied in tests (2), (5) and (6) reveal, (a) that the Untouchables do not receive the mantra from a Brahmin; (b) that the Untouchables are not served by good Brahmin priests at all; and (c) that Untouchables have their own priests reared from themselves. On these facts the Census Commissioners of all provinces are unanimous.[12]

Of the three questions the third is the most important. Unfortunately the Census Commissioner did not realize this. For in making his inquiries he failed to go to the root of the matter to find out: Why were the Untouchables not receiving the mantra from the Brahmin? Why did Brahmins not serve the Untouchables as their family priests? Why do the Untouchables prefer to have their own priests? It is the 'why' of these facts which is more important than the existence of these facts. It is the 'why' of these facts which must be investigated. For the clue to the origin of Untouchability lies hidden behind it.

Before entering upon this investigation, it must be pointed out that the inquiries by the Census Commissioner were in a sense one-sided. They showed that the Brahmins shunned the Untouchables. They did not bring to light the fact that the Untouchables also shunned the Brahmins. Nonetheless, it is a fact. People are so much accustomed to thinking that the Brahmin is the superior of the Untouchable and that the Untouchable accepts himself as his inferior; that this statement that the Untouchables look upon the Brahmin as an impure person is sure to come to them as a matter of great surprise. The fact has however been noted by many writers who have observed and examined the social customs of the Untouchables. To remove any doubt on the point, attention is drawn to the following extracts from their writings.

The fact was noticed by Abbé Dubois who says:[13]

> Even to this day a Pariah is not allowed to pass a Brahmin Street in a village, though nobody can prevent, or prevents, his approaching or passing by a Brahmin's house in towns. The Pariahs, on their part will under no circumstances, allow a Brahmin to pass through their *paracherries* (collection of Pariah huts) as they firmly believe it will lead to their ruin.

Mr [F.R.] Hemingway, the Editor of the *Gazetteer* of the Tanjore District says:

> These castes (Parayan and Pallan or Chakkiliyan[14] castes of Tanjore District) strongly object to the entrance of a Brahmin into their quarters believing that harm will result to them there from.[15]

Speaking of the Holeyas[16] of the Hasan District of Mysore, Captain J.S.F. Mackenzie[17] says:

> Every village has its Holegéri (as the quarters inhabited by the Holeyars is called), outside the village boundary hedge. This, I thought was because they were considered as impure race, whose touch carries defilement with it. Such is the reason generally given by the Brahman, who refuse to receive anything directly from the hands of a Holeyar. And yet the Brahmans consider great luck will wait upon them if they can manage to pass through the Holegéri without being molested. To this Holeyars have a strong objection, and,

> should a Brahmin attempt to enter their quarters, they turn out in a body and slipper him, in former times it is said to death. Members of the other castes may come as far as the door, but they must not (for that would bring the Holeyar bad luck) enter the house. If, by chance, a person happens to get in, the owner takes care to tear the intruder's cloth, tie up some salt in one corner of it, and turn him out. This is supposed to neutralise all the good luck which might have accrued to the trespasser and avert any evil which ought to have befallen the owner of the house.[18]

What is the explanation of this strange phenomenon? The explanation must of course fit in with the situation as it stood at the start, i.e. when the Untouchables were not Untouchables but were only Broken Men.[19] We must ask why the Brahmins refused to officiate at the religious ceremonies of the Broken Men. Is it the case that the Brahmins refused to officiate? Or is it that the Broken Men refused to invite them? Why did the Brahmins regard Broken Men as impure? Why did the Broken Men regard the Brahmins as impure? What is the basis of this antipathy?

This antipathy can be explained through one hypothesis. It is that the Broken Men were Buddhists. As such they did not revere the Brahmins, did not employ them as their priests and regarded them as impure. The Brahmin on the other hand disliked the Broken Men because they were Buddhists and preached against them contempt and hatred with the result that the Broken Men came to be regarded as Untouchables.

We have no direct evidence that the Broken Men were Buddhists. No evidence is as a matter of fact necessary when the majority of Hindus were Buddhists.[20] We may take it that they were.

That there existed hatred and abhorrence against the Buddhists in the mind of the Hindus and that this feeling was created by the

Brahmins is not without support.

Nilakantha[21] in his *Prayaschit Mayukha*[22] quotes a verse from Manu which says: 'If a person touches a Buddhist or a flower of Pachupat, Lokayala, Nastika and Mahapataki, he shall purify himself by a bath.'

The same doctrine is preached by Apararka[23] in his Smriti.[24] *Vrddha Harita*[25] goes further and declares entry into the Buddhist temple as sin requiring a purificatory bath for removing the impurity.

How widespread had become this spirit of hatred and contempt against the followers of Buddha can be observed from the scenes depicted in Sanskrit dramas.[26] The most striking illustration of this attitude towards the Buddhists is to be found in the *Mricchakatika*.[27] In Act VII of that drama the hero Charudatta and his friend Maitreya are shown waiting for Vasantasena in the park outside the city. She fails to turn up and Charudatta decides to leave the park. As they are leaving, they see the Buddhist monk by name Samvahaka. On seeing him, Charudatta says:

> Friend Maitreya, I am anxious to meet Vasantsena ...
>
> Come, let us go. (*After walking a little*) Ah! Here's an inauspicious sight, a Buddhist monk coming towards us. (*After a little reflection*) Well, let him come this way, we shall follow this other path. (*Exit.*)

In Act VIII, the monk is in the park of Sakara, the king's brother-in-law, washing his clothes in a pool. Sakara, accompanied by Vita, turns up and threatens to kill the monk. The following conversation between them is revealing:

> Sakara: Stay, you wicked monk.
>
> Monk: Ah! Here's the king's brother-in-law! Because some monk has offended him, he now beats up any monk he happens to meet.

Sakara: Stay, I will now break your head as one breaks a radish in a tavern. *(Beats him)*.

Vita: Friend, it is not proper to beat a monk who has put on the saffron-robes, being disgusted with the world.[28]

Monk: (*Welcomes*) Be pleased, lay brother.

Sakara: Friend, see. He is abusing me.

Vita: What does he say?

Sakara: He calls me lay brother (*upasaka*). Am I a barber?

Vita: Oh! He is really praising you as a devotee of the Buddha.

Sakara: Why has he come here?

Monk: To wash these clothes.

Sakara: Ah! You wicked monk. Even I myself do not bathe in this pool; I shall kill you with one stroke.

After a lot of beating, the monk is allowed to go. Here is a Buddhist monk in the midst of the Hindu crowd. He is shunned and avoided. The feeling of disgust against him is so great that the people even shun the road the monk is travelling. The feeling of repulsion is so intense that the entry of the Buddhist was enough to cause the exit of the Hindus. The Buddhist monk is on a par with the Brahmin. A Brahmin is immune from death penalty.[29] He is even free from corporal punishment but the Buddhist monk is beaten and assaulted without remorse, without compunction as though there was nothing wrong in it.

If we accept that the Broken Men were followers of Buddhism and did not care to return to Brahmanism when it became triumphant over Buddhism as easily as others did, we have an explanation for both the questions. It explains why the Untouchables regard the Brahmins as inauspicious, do not employ them as their priest and do not even allow them to enter their quarters. It also explains why the Broken Men came to be regarded as Untouchables. The Broken Men hated the Brahmins because the Brahmins were the enemies of Buddhism and the Brahmins imposed Untouchability upon the Broken Men because they would not leave Buddhism. On this reasoning it is possible to conclude that one of the roots of Untouchability lies in the hatred and contempt which the Brahmins created against those who were Buddhist.[30]

Can the hatred between Buddhism and Brahmanism be taken to be the sole cause why Broken Men became Untouchables? Obviously, it cannot be. The hatred and contempt preached by the Brahmins was directed against Buddhists in general and not against the Broken Men in particular. Since Untouchability stuck to Broken Men only, it is obvious that there was some additional circumstance which has played its part in fastening Untouchability upon the Broken Men. What could that circumstance have been? We must next direct our effort in the direction of ascertaining it.

Chapter X
Beef-eating as the root of Untouchability

We now take up test No. 10 referred to in the circular issued by the Census Commissioner and to which reference has already been made in the previous chapter. The test refers to beef-eating.

The Census Returns show that the meat of the dead cow forms the chief item of food consumed by communities which are generally classified as Untouchable communities. No Hindu community, however low, will touch cow's flesh. On the other hand, there is no community which is really an Untouchable community which has not something to do with the dead cow. Some eat her flesh, some remove the skin, some manufacture articles out of her skin and bones.

From the survey of the Census Commissioner, it is well established that Untouchables eat beef. The question however is: Has beef-eating any relation to the origin of Untouchability? Or is it merely an incident in the economic life of the Untouchables? Can we say that the Broken Men came to be treated as Untouchables because they ate beef? There need be no hesitation in returning an affirmative answer to this question. No other answer is consistent with facts as we know them.

In the first place, we have the fact that the Untouchables, or the main communities which compose them, eat the dead cow and those who eat the dead cow are tainted with Untouchability and no others. The co-relation between Untouchability and the use of the dead cow is so great and so close that the thesis that it is the root of Untouchability seems to be incontrovertible.[1] In the second place if there is anything that separates the Untouchables from the Hindus, it is beef-eating. Even a superficial view of the food taboos of the Hindus will show that there are two taboos regarding food which serve as dividing lines. There is one taboo against meat-eating. It divides Hindus into vegetarians and flesh eaters. There is another taboo which is against beef-eating. It divides Hindus into those who eat cow's flesh and those who do not. From the point of view of Untouchability the first dividing line is of no importance. But the second is. For it completely marks off the Touchables from the Untouchables. The Touchables whether they are vegetarians or flesh-eaters are united in their objection to eat cow's flesh. As against them stand the Untouchables who eat cow's flesh without compunction and as a matter of course and habit.[2]

In this context it is not far-fetched to suggest that those who have a nausea against beef-eating should treat those who eat beef as Untouchables. There is really no necessity to enter upon any speculation as to whether beef-eating was or was not the principal reason for the rise of Untouchability. This new theory receives support from the Hindu Shastras. The *Veda Vyas Smriti*[3] contains the following verse which specifies the communities which are included in the category of Antyajas and the reasons why they were so included.[4]

> 2.12–13: The *Charmakars* (cobbler), the *Bhatta* (soldier), the *Bhilla,* the *Rajaka* (washerman), the *Puskara,* the *Nata* (actor), the *Vrata,* the *Meda,* the *Chandala,* the *Dasa,* the *Svapaka,* and the *Kolika*—these are known as Antyajas as well as others who eat cow's flesh.

Generally speaking the smritikars never care to explain the why and the how of their dogmas. But this case is [an] exception. For in this case, Veda Vyas does explain the cause of Untouchability. The clause 'as well as others who eat cow's flesh' is very important. It shows that the smritikars knew that the origin of Untouchability is to be found in the eating of beef. The dictum of Veda Vyas must close the argument. It comes, so to say, straight from the horse's mouth and what is important is that it is also rational for it accords with facts as we know them.

The new approach in the search for the origin of Untouchability has brought to the surface two sources of the origin of Untouchability. One is the general atmosphere of scorn and contempt spread by the Brahmins against those who were Buddhists and the second is the habit of beef-eating kept on by the Broken Men. As has been said, the first circumstance could not be sufficient to account for the stigma of Untouchability attaching itself to the Broken Men. For the scorn and contempt for Buddhists spread by the Brahmins was too general and affected all Buddhists and not merely the Broken Men. The reason why Broken Men only became Untouchables was because in addition to being Buddhists they retained their habit of beef-eating which gave additional ground for offence to the Brahmins to carry their newfound love and reverence to the cow to its logical conclusion. We may therefore conclude that [while] the Broken Men were exposed to scorn and contempt on the ground that they were Buddhists, the main cause of their Untouchability was beef-eating.

The theory of beef-eating as the cause of untouchability also gives rise to many questions. Critics are sure to ask: What is the cause of the nausea which the Hindus have against beef-eating? Were the Hindus always opposed to beef-eating? If not, why did they develop such a nausea against it? Were the Untouchables given to beef-eating from the very start? Why did they not give up beef-eating when it was abandoned by the Hindus? Were the Untouchables always Untouchables? If there was a time when the Untouchables were not Untouchables even though they ate beef why should beef-eating give rise to Untouchability at a later stage? If the Hindus were eating beef, when did they give it up? If Untouchability is a reflex of the nausea of the Hindus against beef-eating, how long after the Hindus had given up beef-eating did Untouchability come into being? These questions must be answered. Without an answer to these questions, the theory will remain under a cloud. It will be considered as plausible but may not be accepted as conclusive. Having put forth the theory, I am bound to answer these questions. I propose to take up the following heads:

1. Did the Hindus never eat beef?
2. What led the Hindus to give up beef-eating?
3. What led the Brahmins to become vegetarians?
4. Why did beef-eating give rise to Untouchability? And
5. When was Untouchability born?

Part V

THE NEW THEORIES AND SOME HARD QUESTIONS

Chapter XI
Did the Hindus never eat beef?

To the question whether the Hindus ever ate beef, every Touchable Hindu, whether he is a Brahmin or a non-Brahmin, will say 'no, never'. In a certain sense, he is right. From times [sic], no Hindu has eaten beef. If this is all that the Touchable Hindu wants to convey by his answer there need be no quarrel over it. But when the learned Brahmins argue that the Hindus not only never ate beef but they always held the cow to be sacred and were always opposed to the killing of the cow, it is impossible to accept their view.

What is the evidence in support of the construction that the Hindus never ate beef and were opposed to the killing of the cow?

There are two series of references in the Rig Veda[1] on which reliance is placed. In one of these, the cow is spoken of as *Aghnya*. They are Rig Veda I.164.27;[2] IV.1.6;[3] V.82.8;[4] VII.69.71;[5] X.87.[6] Aghnya means 'one who does not deserve to be killed'. From this, it is argued that this was a prohibition against the killing of the cow and that since the Vedas are the final authority in the matter of religion, it is concluded that the Aryans could not have killed cows, much less could they have eaten beef. In another series of references the cow is spoken of as sacred. They are Rig Veda VI.28.1.8[7] and VIII.101.15.[8] In these verses the cow is addressed as Mother of Rudras, the Daughter of Vasus, the Sister of the Adityas and the Centre of Nectar. Another reference on the subject is in Rig Veda VIII.101.16 where the cow is called Devi (Goddess).

Reliance is also placed on certain passages in the Brahmanas and Sutras. There are two passages in the *Satapatha Brahmana*[9] which relate to animal sacrifice and beef-eating. One is at III.1.2.21 and reads as follows:

> He (the Adhvaryu) then makes him enter the hall. Let him not eat (the flesh) of either the cow or the ox, for the cow and the ox doubtless support everything here on earth. The gods spake, 'Verily, the cow and the ox support everything here: come, let us bestow on the cow and the ox whatever vigour belongs to other species (of animals)' [...] and therefore the cow and the ox eat most. Hence were one to eat (the flesh) of an ox or a cow, there would be, as it were, an eating of everything, or, as it were, a going to the end (or, to destruction). ... Let him therefore not eat (the flesh) of the cow and the ox.

The other passage is at I.2.3.6.[10] It speaks against animal sacrifice and on ethical grounds. A similar statement is contained in the *Apastamba Dharma Sutra*[11] at I.5.17.29.[12] Apastamba lays a general embargo on the eating of cow's flesh. Such is the evidence in support of the contention that the Hindus never ate beef. What conclusion can be drawn from this evidence? So far as the evidence from the Rig Veda is concerned the conclusion is based on a misreading and misunderstanding of the texts. The adjective Aghnya applied to the cow in the *Rig Veda* means a cow that was yielding milk and therefore not fit for being killed.[13]

That the cow is venerated in the Rig Veda is of course true. But this regard and veneration of the cow are only to be expected from an agricultural community like the Indo-Aryans. This application of the utility of the cow did not prevent the Aryan from killing the cow for purposes of food. Indeed the cow was killed because the cow was regarded as sacred. As observed by Mr Kane:[14] 'It was not that the cow was not sacred in Vedic times, it was because of her sacredness that it is ordained in the *Vajasaneyi Samhita*[15] that beef should be eaten.'[16]

That the Aryans of the Rig Veda did kill cows for purposes of food and ate beef is abundantly clear from the Rig Veda itself. In the Rig Veda (X.86.14),[17] Indra says: 'They cook for one fifteen plus twenty oxen'. The Rig Veda (X.91.14)[18] says that for Agni were sacrificed horses, bulls, oxen, barren cows and rams. From the Rig Veda (X.72.6)[19] it appears that the cow was killed with a sword or axe. As to the testimony of the *Satapatha Brahmana*, can it be said to be conclusive? Obviously, it cannot be. For there are passages in the other Brahmanas which give a different opinion.

To give only one instance. Among the *Kamyashtis*[20] set forth in the *Taittiriya Brahmana*,[21] not only the sacrifice of oxen and cows are laid down, but we are even told what kind and description of oxen and cows are to be offered to what deities. Thus, a dwarf ox is to be chosen for sacrifice to Vishnu; a drooping horned bull with a blaze on the forehead to Indra as the destroyer of Vritra; a black cow to Pushan; a red cow to Rudra; and so on. The *Taittiriya Brahmana* notes another sacrifice called *Panchasaradiyaseva*, the most important element of which was the immolation of seventeen five-year old humpless, dwarf-bulls, and as many dwarf heifers under three years old.

As against the statement of the *Apastamba Dharma Sutra*, the following points may be noted. First is the contrary statement contained in that very Sutra. At 14.15.29, the Sutra says: 'The cow and the bull are sacred and therefore should be eaten.'[22]

The second is the prescription of Madhuparka[23] contained in the Grihya Sutras.[24] Among the Aryans the etiquette for receiving important guests had become settled into custom and had become a ceremony. The most important offering was Madhuparka. [D] etailed descriptions regarding Madhuparka are to be found in the various Grihya Sutras. According to most of the Grihya Sutras there are six persons who have a right to be served with Madhuparka namely; (1) Ritvija or the Brahmin called to perform a sacrifice, (2) Acharya, the teacher, (3) The bridegroom, (4) The king, (5) The Snataka, the student who has just finished his studies at the Gurukul, and (6) Any person who is dear to the host. Some add Atithi[25] to this list. Except in the case of Ritvija, king and Acharya, Madhuparka is to be offered to the rest once in a year. To the Ritvija, king and Acharya it is to be offered each time they come.

What was this Madhuparka made of?

> There is divergence about the substances mixed in offering Madhuparka. Asv.gr[26] and Ap.gr. (13.10)[27] prescribe a mixture of honey and curds or clarified butter and curds. Others like Par.gr. 13[28] prescribe a mixture of three (curds, honey and butter). Ap.gr. (13.11–12) states the view of some that those three may be mixed or five (those three with fried yava grain and barley). Hir.gr. I, 12, 10–12 give the option of mixing three of five (curds, honey, ghee, water and ground grain). The *Kausika Sutra*[29] (92) speaks of nine kinds of mixtures, viz., Brahma (honey and curds), Aindra (of payasa), Saumya (curds and ghee), Pausna (ghee and mantha), Sarasvata (milk and ghee), Mausala (wine and ghee, this being used only in Sautramanai and Rajasuya sacrifices), Parivrajaka (sesame oil and oil cake). The Madhava[30] gr I.9.22 says that the Veda declares that the Madhuparka must not be without flesh and so it recommends that if the cow is let loose, goat's meat or payasa (rice cooked in milk) may be offered; the Hir.gr. I.13, 14 says that other meat should be offered; Baud. gr. (I.2,51–54) says that when the cow is let off, the flesh of a goat or ram may be offered or some forest flesh (of a deer, etc.)

may be offered, as there can be no Madhuparka without flesh or if one is unable to offer flesh one may cook ground grains.[31]

Thus the essential element in Madhuparka is flesh and particularly cow's flesh.

The killing of cow for the guest had grown to such an extent that the guest came to be called 'Go-ghna'[32] which means the killer of the cow. To avoid this slaughter of the cows the *Asvalayana Grahya Sutra*[33] (1.24.25) suggests that the cow should be let loose when the guest comes so as to escape the rule of etiquette.

Thirdly, reference may be made to the ritual relating to disposal of the dead to counter the testimony of the *Apastamba Dharma Sutra*.[34] The Sutra says:

2. He should then put the following (sacrificial) implements (on the dead body)
3. Into the right hand the (spoon called) Guhu.
4. Into the left the (other spoon called) Upabhrit.
5. On his right side the (wooden sacrificial sword called) Sphya, on his left (side) the Agnihotrahavani (i.e., the ladle with which the Agnihotra oblations are sacrifi[c]ed).
6. On his chest the (big sacrificial ladle called) Dhruva. On his head the dishes. On his teeth the pressing-stones.
7. On the two sides of his nose, the two (smaller sacrificial ladles called) Sruvas.
8. Or, if there is only one (Sruva), breaking it (in two pieces).
9. On his two ears the two Prasitraharanas (i.e. the vessels into which the portion of the sacrificial food belonging to the Brahmin) is put.
10. Or, if there is only one (Prasitraharana), breaking it (in two pieces).
11. On his belly the (vessel called) Patri.

12. And the cup into which the cut-off portion (of the sacrificial food) are put.
13. On his secret parts the (staff called) Samy[a].
14. On his thighs two kindling woods.
15. On his legs the mortar and the pestle.
16. On his feet the two baskets.
17. Or, if there is only one (basket), breaking it in two pieces.
18. Those (of the implements) which have a hollow (into which liquids can be poured) are filled with sprinkled butter.
19. The son (of the deceased person) should take the under and the upper mill-stone for himself.
20. And the implements made of copper, iron and earthenware.
21. Taking out the omentum of the she-animal he should cover therewith the head and the mouth (of the dead person) with the verse, '[P]ut on the armour (which will protect thee) against Agni, by (that which comes from) the cows' (Rig Veda X.16.7).
22. Taking out the kidneys (of the animal) he should lay them into the hands (of the dead body) with the verse, '[E]scape the two hounds, the sons of Sar[a]ma (Rig Veda X.14.10), the right (kidney) into the right (hand) and the left into the left hand.
22. The heart (of the animal he puts) on the heart (of the deceased).
23. And two lumps (of flour or rice), according to some (teachers).
24. (Only) if there are no kidneys, according to some (teachers).
25. Having distributed the whole (animal), limb by limb (placing its different limbs on the corresponding limbs of the deceased) and having covered it with its hide, he recites, when the Pranita water is carried forward, (the verse), 'Agni, do not overturn this cup' (Rig Veda X.16.8).
26. Bending his left knee he should sacrifice Agya oblation[s] into the Dakshina fire with (the formulas), 'To Agni svaha! [T]o

Kama svaha! [T]o the world svaha! [T]o Anumati Svaha.'

27. A fifth (oblation) on the chest of the deceased with (the formula), '[F]rom this one verily thou hast been born. May he now be born out of thee, N.N! To the heaven worlds Svaha.'

From the *Asvalayana Grihya Sutra* it is clear that among the ancient Indo-Aryans when a person died, an animal had to be killed and parts of the animal were placed on the appropriate parts of the dead body before the dead body was burned. Such is the state of the evidence on the subject of cow-killing and beef-eating. Which part of it is to be accepted as true? The correct view is that the testimony of the *Satapatha Brahmana* and the *Apastamba Dharma Sutra* in so far as it supports the view that Hindus were against cow-killing and beef-eating, are merely exhortations against the excesses of cow-killing and not prohibitions against cow-killing. Indeed the exhortations prove that cow-killing and eating of beef had become a common practice. That notwithstanding these exhortations cow-killing and beef-eating continued. That most often they fell on deaf ears is proved by the conduct of Yajnavalkya,[35] the great Rishi of the Aryans. The first passage quoted above from the *Satapatha Brahmana* was really addressed to Yajnavalkya as an exhortation. How did Yajnavalkya respond? After listening to the exhortation this is what Yajnavalkya said: 'I, for one, eat it, provided that it is tender.'[36]

That the Hindus at one time did kill cows and did eat beef is proved abundantly by the description of the Yajnas given in the Buddhist Sutras which relate to periods much later than the Vedas and the Brahmanas. The scale on which the slaughter of cows and animals took place was colossal. It is not possible to give a total of such slaughter on all accounts committed by the Brahmins in the name of religion. Some idea of the extent of this slaughter can however be had from references to it in Buddhist literature. As an illustration reference may be made to the "Kutadanta Sutta"[37] in which Buddha preached against the performance of animal sacrifices to the Brahmin Kutadanta.[38] Buddha, though speaking in a tone of sarcastic travesty, gives a good idea of the practices and rituals of the Vedic sacrifices when he said:

> And further, O Brahman, at that sacrifice neither were any oxen slain, neither goats, nor fowls, nor fatted pigs, nor were any kind of living creatures put to death. No trees were cut down to be used as posts, no Dabbha grasses mown to strew around the sacrificial spot. And the slaves and messengers and workmen there employed were driven neither by rods nor fear, nor carried on their work weeping with tears upon their faces.[39]

Kutadanta on the other hand in thanking Buddha for his conversion gives an idea of the magnitude of the slaughter of animals which took place at such sacrifices when he says:

> I, even I betake myself to the venerable Gotama as my guide, to the Doctrine and the Order. May the venerable One accept me as a disciple, as one who, from this day forth, as long as life endures, has taken him as his guide. And I myself, O, Gotama, will have the seven hundred bulls, and the seven hundred steers, and the seven hundred heifers, and the seven hundred goats, and the seven hundred rams set free. To them I grant their life. Let them eat grass and drink fresh water and may cool breezes waft around them.[40]

In the *Samyutta Nikaya* (III,1–9)[41] we have another description of a Yajna performed by Pasenadi, king of Kosala. It is said that five hundred bulls, five hundred calves and many heifers, goats and rams were led to the pillar to be sacrificed.

With this evidence no one can doubt that there was a time when Hindus—both Brahmins and non-Brahmins—ate not only flesh but also beef.

Chapter XII
Why did non-Brahmins give up beef-eating?

I

The food habits of the different classes of Hindus have been as fixed and stratified as their cults. Just as Hindus can be classified on their basis of their cults so also they can be classified on the basis of their habits of food. On the basis of their cults, Hindus are either Saivites (followers of Siva) or Vaishnavites (followers of Vishnu).[1] Similarly, Hindus are either Mansahari (those who eat flesh) or Shakahari (those who are vegetarians).

For ordinary purposes the division of Hindus into two classes Mansahari and Shakahari may be enough. But it must be admitted that it is not exhaustive and does not take account of all the classes which exist in Hindu society. For an exhaustive classification, the class of Hindus called Mansahari shall have to be further divided into two sub-classes: (i) Those who eat flesh but do not eat cow's flesh; and (ii) Those who eat flesh including cow's flesh; In other words, on the basis of food taboos, Hindu society falls into three classes : (i) Those who are vegetarians; (ii) Those who eat flesh but do not eat cow's flesh; and (iii) Those who eat flesh including cow's flesh. Corresponding to this classification, we have in Hindu society three classes: (1) Brahmins; (2) non-Brahmins; and (3) The Untouchables. This division though not in accord with the fourfold division of society called Chaturvarnya, yet it is in accord with facts as they exist. For, in the Brahmins[2] we have a class which is vegetarian, in the non-Brahmins the class which eats flesh but does not eat cow's flesh and in the Untouchables a class which eats flesh including cow's flesh.

This threefold division is therefore substantial and is in accord with facts. Anyone who stops to turn over this classification in his mind is bound to be struck by the position of the non-Brahmins. One can quite understand vegetarianism. One can quite understand meat-eating. But it is difficult to understand why a person who is a flesh-eater should object to one kind of flesh namely cow's flesh. This is an anomaly which calls for explanation. Why did the non-Brahmin give up beef-eating? For this purpose it is necessary to examine laws on the subject. The relevant legislation must be found either in the Law of Asoka or the Law of Manu.

II

To begin with Asoka.[3] The edicts of Asoka which have reference to this matter are Rock Edict No. I[4] and Pillar Edict Nos. II and V[5]. Rock Edict No. I[6] reads as follows:

> This pious Edict has been written by command of His Sacred and Gracious Majesty the King.
>
> Here [in the capital] no animal may be slaughtered for sacrifice, nor may the holiday-feast be held, because His Sacred and Gracious Majesty, the King sees much offence in the holiday feast, although in certain places holiday-feasts are excellent in the sight of His Sacred and Gracious Majesty the King.
>
> Formerly, in the kitchen of His Sacred and Gracious Majesty the King each day many hundred thousands of living creatures were slaughtered to make curries. But now, when this pious edict is being written, only three living creatures are slaughtered [daily] for curry, to wit, two peacocks and one

antelope—the antelope, however, not invariably. Even those three living creatures henceforth shall not be slaughtered.

Pillar Edict No. II is in the following terms:[7]

> Thus saith His Sacred and Gracious Majesty, the King: "The Law of Piety is excellent." But wherein consists the Law of Piety? In these things, to wit, little impiety, many good deeds, compassion, liberality, truthfulness and purity. The gift of spiritual insight I have given in manifold ways; whilst on two-footed and four-footed beings, on birds and the denizens of the waters, I have conferred various favours—even unto the boon of life; and many other good deeds have I done. For this my purpose have I caused this pious edict to be written, that men may walk after its teaching, and that it may long endure; and he who will follow its teaching will do well.

Pillar Edict V says:[8]

> Thus saith His Sacred and Gracious Majesty the King: When I had been consecrated twenty-six years the following species were declared *exempt from slaughter,*[9] namely: Parrots, starlings (?) adjutants, "Brahmany ducks", geese, *nandimukhas, gelatas,* bats, queen-ants, female tortoises, "boneless fish", *vedaveyakas, gangapuputakas,* (?) skate, (river) tortoises, porcupines, tree-squirrels, (?) *barasingha* stag, "Brahmany bulls", (?) monkeys, rhinoceros, grey doves, village pigeons, and *all four-footed animals which are not utilised or eaten.*[10] She-goats, ewes, and sows, that is to say, those either with young or in milk, are exempt from slaughter as well as their off-spring up to six months of age.
>
> The caponing of cocks must not be done.
>
> Chaff must not be burned along with the living things in it.
>
> Forests must not be burned either for mischief or so as to destroy living creatures.

The living must not be fed with the living. At each of the three seasonal full moons, and at the full moon of the month Tishya (December–January), for three days in each case, namely the fourteenth and fifteenth days of the first fortnight, and the first day of the second fortnight, as well as on the fast days throughout the year, fish is exempt from killing and may not be sold.

On the same days, in elephant-preserves or fish-ponds no other classes of animals may be destroyed.

On the eighth, fourteenth, and fifteenth days of each fortnight, as well as on the Tishya and Punarvasa[11] days and festival days, the castration of bulls must not be performed, nor may he-goats, rams, boars and other animals liable to castration be castrated.

On the Tishya and Punarvasa days, on the seasonal full moon days, and during the fortnights of the seasonal full moons the branding of horses and oxen must not be done.

During the time up to the twenty-sixth anniversary of my consecration twenty-five jail deliveries have been effected.

So much for the legislation of Asoka.

III

Let us turn to Manu.[12] His Laws contain the following provisions regarding meat-eating:[13]

V.11. Let him avoid all carnivorous birds and those living in villages, and one-hoofed animals which are not specially permitted (to be eaten), and the Tittibha (Parra Jacana).

V.12. The sparrow, the Plava, the Hamsa, the Brahmani duck, the village-cock, the Sarasa crane, the Raggudala, the woodpecker, the parrot, and the starling.

V.13. Those which feed striking with their beaks, web-footed birds, the Koyashti, those which scratch with their toes, those which dive and live on fish, meat from a slaughter-house and dried meat.

V.14. The Baka and the Balaka crane, the raven, the Khangarilaka (animals) that eat fish, village-pigs, and all kinds of fishes.

V.15. He who eats the flesh of any (animal) is called the eater of the flesh of that (particular creature), he who eats fish is an eater of every (kind of) flesh; let him therefore avoid fish.

V.16. (But the fish called) Pathina and (that called) Rohita may be eaten, if used for offering to the gods or to the manes; (one may eat) likewise Ragivas, Simhatundas, and Sasalkas on all (occasions).

V.17. Let him not eat solitary or unknown beasts and birds, though they may fall under (the categories of) eatable (creatures), nor any five-toed (animals).

V.18. The porcupine, the hedgehog, the iguana, the rhinoceros, the tortoise, and the hare they declare to be eatable; likewise those (domestic animals) that have teeth in one jaw excepting camels.

IV

Here is the survey of the legislation both by Asoka and by Manu on the slaughter of animals. We are of course principally concerned with the cow. Examining the legislation of Asoka the question is: Did he prohibit the killing of the cow? On this issue there seems to be a difference of opinion. Prof Vincent Smith is of opinion that Asoka did not prohibit the killing of the cow. Commenting on the legislation of Asoka on the subject, Prof Smith says: 'It is noteworthy that Asoka's rules do not forbid the slaughter of cow, which, apparently, continued to be lawful.'[14]

Prof Radhakumud Mookerji joins issue with Prof Smith and says[15] that Asoka did prohibit the slaughter of the cow. Prof Mookerji relies upon the reference in Pillar Edict V to the rule of exemption which was made applicable to all four-footed animals and argues that under this rule cow was exempted from killing. This is not a correct reading of the statement in the Edict. The statement in the Edict is a qualified statement. It does not refer to all four-footed animals but only to four-footed animals, '*which are not utilised or eaten*'. A cow cannot be said to be a four-footed animal which was not utilized or eaten. Prof Vincent Smith seems to be correct in saying that Asoka did not prohibit the slaughter of the cow. Prof Mookerji tries to get out of the difficulty by saying that at the time of Asoka the cow was not eaten and therefore came within the prohibition. His statement is simply absurd for the cow was an animal which was very much eaten by all classes.

It is quite unnecessary to resort as does Prof Mookerji to a forced construction of the Edict and to make Asoka prohibit the slaughter of the cow as though it was his duty to do so. Asoka had no particular interest in the cow and owed no special duty to protect her against killing. Asoka was interested in the sanctity of all life human as well as animal. He felt [it] his duty to prohibit the taking of life where taking of life was not necessary. That is why he prohibited slaughtering animal for sacrifice which he regarded as unnecessary and of animals which are not utilized nor eaten which again would be wanton and unnecessary. That he did not prohibit the slaughter of the cow in specie may well be taken as a fact which for having regard to the Buddhist attitude in the matter cannot be used against Asoka as a ground for casting blame.

Coming to Manu there is no doubt that he too did not prohibit the slaughter of the cow. On the other hand he made the eating of cow's flesh on certain occasions obligatory.

Why then did the non-Brahmins give up eating beef? There appears to be no apparent reason for this departure on their part. But there must be some reason behind it. The reason I like to suggest is that it was due to their desire to imitate the Brahmins that the non-Brahmins gave up beef-eating. This may be a novel theory but it is not an impossible theory. As the French author, Gabriel Tarde[16] has explained that culture within a society spreads by imitation of the ways and manners of the superior classes by the inferior classes. This imitation is so regular in its flow that its working is as mechanical as the working of a natural law. Gabriel Tarde speaks of the laws of imitation. One of these laws is that the lower classes always imitate the higher classes. This is a matter of such common knowledge that hardly any individual can be found to question its validity.

That the spread of cow-worship among and cessation of beef-eating by the non-Brahmins has taken place by reason of the habit of the non-Brahmins to imitate the Brahmins who were undoubtedly their superiors is beyond dispute. Of course there was an extensive propaganda in favour of cow-worship by the Brahmins. The *Gayatri Purana*[17] is a piece of this propaganda. But initially it is the result of the natural law of imitation. This, of course, raises another question: Why did the Brahmins give up beef-eating?

Chapter XIII
What made the Brahmins become vegetarians?

I

The non-Brahmins have evidently undergone a revolution. From being beef-eaters to have become non-beef-eaters was indeed a revolution. But if the non-Brahmins underwent one revolution, the Brahmins had undergone two. They gave up beef-eating which was one revolution. To have given up meat-eating altogether and become vegetarians was another revolution.[1]

That this was a revolution is beyond question. For as has been shown in the previous chapters there was a time when the Brahmins were the greatest beef-eaters. Although the non-Brahmins did eat beef they could not have had it every day. The cow was a costly animal and the non-Brahmins could ill afford to slaughter it just for food. He only did it on special occasion when his religious duty or personal interest to propitiate a deity compelled him to do. But the case with the Brahmin was different. He was a priest. In a period overridden by ritualism there was hardly a day on which there was no cow sacrifice to which the Brahmin was not invited by some non-Brahmin. For the Brahmin every day was a beef-steak day. The Brahmins were therefore the greatest beef-eaters.

The yajna of the Brahmins was nothing but the killing of innocent animals carried on in the name of religion with pomp and ceremony with an attempt to enshroud it in mystery with a view to conceal their appetite for beef. Some idea of this mystery pomp and ceremony can be had from the directions contained in the *Aitareya*

Brahmana[2] touching the killing of animals in a yajna.

The actual killing of the animal is preceded by certain initiatory rites accompanied by incantations too long and too many to be detailed here. It is enough to give an idea of the main features of the sacrifice. The sacrifice commences with the erection of the sacrificial post called the Yupa[3] to which the animal is tied before it is slaughtered. After setting out why the Yupa is necessary the *Aitareya Brahmana* proceeds to state what it stands for. It says:[4]

> This Yupa is a weapon. Its point must have eight edges. For a weapon (or iron club) has eight edges. Whenever he strikes with it an enemy or adversary, he kills him. (This weapon serves) to put down him (every one) who is to be put down by him (the sacrificer). The Yupa is a weapon which stands erected (being ready) to slay an enemy. Thence an enemy (of the sacrificer) who might be present (at the sacrifice) comes of all ill after having seen the Yupa of such or such one.

The selection of the wood to be used for the Yupa is made to vary with the purposes which the sacrificer wishes to achieve by the sacrifice. The *Aitareya Brahmana* says:

> He who desires heaven, ought to make his Yupa of Khadira wood. For the gods conquered the celestial world by means of a Yupa, made of Khadira wood. In the same way the sacrificer conquers the celestial world by means of a Yupa, made of Khadira wood.
>
> He who desires food and wishes to grow fat ought to make his Yupa of Bilva wood. For the Bilva tree bears fruits every year; it is the symbol of fertility; for it increases (every year) in size from the roots up to the branches, therefore it is a symbol of fatness. He who having such [a] knowledge makes his Yupa of Bilva wood, makes fat his children and cattle.
>
> As regards the Yupa made of Bilva wood (it is further to

be remarked), that they call 'light' *bilva*. He who has such a knowledge becomes a light among his own people, the most distinguished among his own people.

He who desires beauty and sacred knowledge ought to make his Yupa of Palasa wood. For the Palasa is among the trees [of] beauty and sacred knowledge. He who having such a knowledge makes his Yupa of Palasa wood, becomes beautiful and acquires sacred knowledge.

As regards the Yupa made of Palasa wood (there is further to be remarked), that the Palasa is the womb of all trees. Thence they speak on account of the *palasam* (foliage) [of the Palasa tree, of the *palasam*] of this or that tree (i.e. they call the foliage of every tree *palasam*). He who has such knowledge obtains (the gratification of) any desire, he might have regarding all trees (i.e. he obtains from all trees anything he might wish for).

This is followed by the ceremony of anointing the sacrificial post.[5]

The Adhvaryu says (to the Hotar[6]): "We anoint the sacrificial post (Yupa); repeat the mantra (required)". The Hotar then repeats the verse: "Amjanti tvam adhvare" (3, 8, 1), i.e. "The priests anoint thee, O tree! with celestial honey (butter); provide (us) with wealth if thou standest here erected, or if thou art lying on thy mother (earth)." The "celestial honey" is the melted butter (with which the priests anoint the Yupa). (The second half verse from) "provide us" &c. means: "thou mayest stand or lie, provide us with wealth.

[...]

(The Hotar then repeats :) "jato jayate sudinatve" &c. (3, 8, 5) i.e. "After having been born, he (the Yupa) is growing (to serve) in the prime of his life the sacrifice of mortal men. The wise are busy in decorating (him, the Yupa) with skill.

He, as an eloquent messenger of the gods, lifts his voice (that it might be heard by the gods)." He (the Yupa) is called jata, i.e., born, because he is born by this (by the recital of the first quarter of this verse). (By the word) vardhamana, i.e. growing, they make him (the Yupa) grow in this manner. (By the words:) punanti (i.e. to clean, decorate), they clean him in this manner. (By the words:) "he as an eloquent messenger, &c." he announces the Yupa (the fact of his existence), to the gods.

The Hotar then concludes (the ceremony of anointing the sacrificial post) with the verse "yuva suvasah parivitah" (3, 8, 4), i.e. "the youth decorated with ribands, has arrived; he is finer (than all trees) which ever grew; the wise priests raise him up under recital of well-framed thoughts of their mind." The youth decorated with ribands, is the vital air (the soul), which is covered by the limbs of the body. (By the words:) "he is finer," &c. he means that he (the Yupa) is becoming finer (more excellent, beautiful) by this (mantra)."

The next ceremony is the carrying of fire round the sacrificial animal.[7] The *Aitareya Brahmana* gives the following directions on this point. It says:[8]

When the fire is carried round (the animal) the Adhvaryu[9] says to the Hotar: repeat (thy mantras). The Hotar then repeats this triplet of verses, addressed to Agni, and composed in the Gayatri metre: agnir hota no adhvare (4,15,1–3) i.e., (1) Agni, our priest, is carried round about like a horse, he who is among gods, the god of sacrifices, (2) Like a charioteer Agni passes thrice by the sacrifice; to the gods he carries the offering, (3) The master of food, the seer of Agni, went round the offering; he bestows riches on the sacrificer.

When the fire is carried round (the animal) then he makes him (Agni) prosper by means of his own deity and his own metre. 'As a horse he is carried' means: they carry him as if he were a horse, round about. Like a charioteer Agni passes thrice by the sacrifice means: he goes round the sacrifice like a charioteer (swiftly). He is called *vajapati* (master of food) because he is the master of (different kinds of) food.

The Advaryu says: give Hotar! the additional order for dispatching offerings to the gods.

[...]

The Hotar then says (to the slaughterers): *Ye divine slaughterers, commence* (your work), *as well as ye who are human!* that is to say, he orders all the slaughterers among gods as well as among men (to commence).

Bring hither the instruments for killing, ye who are ordering the sacrifice, in behalf of the two masters of the sacrifice.

The animal is the offering, the sacrificer the master of the offering. Thus he (the Hotar) makes prosper the sacrificer by means of his (the sacrifcer's) own offering. Thence they truly say: for whatever deity the animal is killed, that one is the master of the offering. If the animal is to be offered to one deity only, the priest should say: *medhapataye* 'to the master of the sacrifice (singular)'; if to two deities, then he should use the dual 'to both masters of the offering', and if to several deities, then he should use the plural, 'to the masters of the offering'. This is the established custom.

Bring ye for him fire! For the animal when carried (to the slaughter) saw death before it. Not wishing to go to the gods, the gods said to it: Come we will bring thee to heaven! The animal consented and said: One of you should walk before me.

They consented. Agni then walked before it, and it followed after Agni. Thence they say, every animal belongs to Agni, for it followed after him. Thence they carry before the animal fire (Agni).

Spread the (sacred) grass! The animal lives on herbs. He (the Hotar) thus provides the animal with its entire soul (the herbs being supposed to form part of it).

After the ceremony of carrying fire round the animal comes the delivery of the animal to the priests for sacrifice. Who should offer the animal for sacrifice? On this point the direction of the *Aitareya Brahmana* is—

> *The mother, the father, the brother, sister, friend,* and *companion should give this (animal) up* (for being slaughtered)! When these words are pronounced, they seize the animal which is (regarded as) entirely given up by its relations (parents, &c.)[10]

On reading this direction one wonders why almost everybody is required to join in offering the animal for sacrifice. The reason is simple. There were altogether seventeen Brahmin priests who were entitled to take part in performing the sacrifice.[11] Naturally enough they wanted the whole carcass to themselves.[12] Indeed they could not give enough to each of the seventeen priests unless they had the whole carcass to distribute. Legally the Brahmins could not claim the whole carcass unless everybody who could not claim any right over the animal had been divested of it. Hence the direction requiring even the companion of the sacrificer to take part in offering the animal. Then comes the ceremony of actually killing the animal. The *Aitareya Brahmana* gives the details of the mode and manner of killing the animal. Its directions are:[13]

> *Turn its feet northwards! Make its eye to go to the sun, dismiss its breath to the wind, its life to the air, its hearing to the directions, its body to the earth.*

In this way he (the Hotar) places it (connects it) with these worlds.

> *Take off the skin entire (without cutting it). Before operating*

> *the naval, tear out omentum! Stop its breathing within* (by stopping its mouth)! Thus he (the Hotar) puts its breath in the animals.
>
> *Make of its breast a piece like an eagle, of its arms* (two pieces like) *two hatchets, of its forearms* (two pieces like) *two spikes, of its shoulders* (two pieces like) *two kashyapas, its loins should be unbroken* (entire); (make of) *its thighs* (two pieces like) *two shields, of the two kneepans* (two pieces like) *two oleander leaves; take out its twenty six ribs according to their order; preserve every limb of it in its integrity.* Thus he benefits all its limbs.

There remain two ceremonies to complete the sacrificial killing of the animal. One is to absolve the Brahmin priests who played the butcher's part. Theoretically they are guilty of murder for the animal is only a substitute for the sacrificer. To absolve them from the consequences of murder, the Hotar is directed by the *Aitareya Brahmana* to observe the following injunction:[14]

> *Do not cut the entrails which resemble an owl* (when taking out the omentum), *nor should among your children, O slaughterers! or among their offspring any one be found who might cut them.* By speaking these words, he presents these entrails to the slaughterers among the gods as well as to those among men.
>
> The Hotar shall then say thrice: O *Adhrigu* (and ye others), *kill* (the animal), *do it well;* kill it, O *Adhrigu.*
>
> [...]
>
> After the animal has been killed, (he should say thrice:) *Far may it* (the consequences of murder) be (from us). For *Adhrigu*[15] among the gods is he who silences (the animal) and the *Apapa*[16] (away, away!) is he who puts it down. By speaking those words he surrenders the animal to those who silence it (by stopping its mouth) and to those who butcher it.

> The Hotar then mutters (he makes, *japa*[17]); 'O slaughterers! may all good you might do abide by us! and all mischief you might do go elsewhere!' The Hotar gives by (this) speech the order (for killing the animal), for Agni had given the order for killing (the animal) with the same words when he was the Hotar of the gods.
>
> By those words (the *japa* mentioned) the Hotar removes (all evil consequences) from those who suffocate the animal and those who butcher it, in all that they might transgress the rule by cutting one piece too soon, the other too late, or by cutting a too large, or a too small piece. The Hotar enjoying this happiness clears himself (from all guilt), and attains the full length of his life (and it serves the sacrificer) for obtaining his full life. He who has such a knowledge, attains the full length of his life.

The *Aitareya Bramhana* next deals with the question of disposing of the parts of the dead animal. In this connection its direction is—[18]

> *Dig a ditch in the earth to hide its excrements.* The excrements consist of vegetable food; for the earth is the place for the herbs. Thus the Hotar puts them (the excrements) finally in their proper places.
>
> *Present the evil spirits with the blood!* For the gods having deprived (once) the evil spirits of their share in the Haviryajnas[19] (such as the Full and New Moon offerings) apportioned to them the husks and smallest grains, and after having them turned out of the great sacrifice (such as the Soma and animal sacrifices), presented to them the blood. Thence the Hotar pronounces the words: *present the evil spirits with the blood!* By giving them this share he deprives the evil spirits of any other share in the sacrifice. They say: one should not address the evil spirits in the sacrifice, any

evil spirits whichever they might be (Rakshasa, Asuras, &c.); for the sacrifice is to be without the evil spirits (not to be disturbed by them). But others say: one should address them; for who deprives any one, entitled to a share, of this share, will be punished (by him whom he deprives); and if he himself does not suffer the penalty, then his son, and if his son be spared, then his grandson will suffer it, and thus he resents on him (the son or grandson) what he wanted to resent on you.

> However, if the Hotar addresses them, he should do so with a low voice. For both, the low voice and the evil spirits, are, as it were, hidden. If he addresses them with a loud voice, then such one speaks in the voice of the evil spirits, and is capable of producing Rakshasa-sounds (a horrible, terrific voice). The voice in which the haughty man and the drunkard speak is that of the evil spirits (Rakshasas). He who has such knowledge will neither himself become haughty nor will such a man be among his offspring.

Then follows the last and the concluding ceremony that of offering parts of the body of the animal to the gods. It is called the Manota. According to the *Aitareya Brahmana*—[20]

> The Adhvaryu [now] says (to the Hotar): recite the verses appropriate to the offering of the parts of the sacrificial animal which are cut off for the Manota. He then repeats the hymn: Thou, O Agni, art the first Manota[21] (6, 1).

There remains the question of sharing the flesh of the animal. On this issue the division was settled by the *Aitareya Brahmana* in the following terms:[22]

> Now follows the division of the different parts of the sacrificial animal (among the priests). We shall describe it. The two jawbones with the tongue are to be given to the Prastotar; the breast in the form of an eagle to the Udgatar; the throat with the palate to the Pratihartar; the lower part of the right loins

to the Hotar: the left to the Brahma; the right thigh to the Maitravaruna; the left to the Brahmanachhamsi; the right side with the shoulder to the Adhvaryu; the left side to those who accompany the chants; the left shoulder to the Pratipashatar; the lower part of the right arm to the Neshtar; the lower part of the left arm to the Potar; the upper of the right thigh to the Achhavaka; the left to the Agnidhara; the upper part of the right arm to the Atreya; the left to the Sadasya; the back bone and the urinal bladder to the Grihapati (sacrificer); the right feet to the Grihapati who gives a feasting; the left feet to the wife of that Grihapati who gives a feasting; the upper lip is common to both (the Grihapati and his wife), which is to be divided by the Grihapati. They offer the tail of the animal to wives, but they should give it to a Brahmana; the fleshy processes *(manikah)* on the neck and three gristles *(kikasah)* to the Gravastut; three other gristles and one-half of the fleshy part on the back *(vaikartta)* to the Unnetar; the other half of the fleshy part on the neck and the left lobe *(kloma)* to the slaughterer, who should present it to a Brahmana, if he himself would not happen to be a Brahmana. The head is to be given to the Subrahmanya, the skin belongs to him (the Subrahmanya), who spoke, *svah sutyam* (tomorrow at the Soma sacrifice); that part of the sacrificial animal at a Soma sacrifice which belongs to Ila (sacrificial food) is common to all the priests; only for the Hotar it is optional.

All these portions of the sacrificial animal amount to thirty-six single pieces, each of which represents the pada (foot) of a verse by which the sacrifice is carried up. The Brihati metre[23] consists of thirty-six syllables; and the heavenly worlds are of the Brihati nature. In this way (by dividing the animal into thirty-six parts) they gain life (in this world) and the heavens, and having become established in both (this and that world)

> they walk there.
>
> To those who divide the sacrificial animal in the way mentioned, it becomes the guide to heaven. But those who make the division otherwise are like scoundrels and miscreants who kill an animal merely (for gratifying their lust after flesh).
>
> This division of the sacrificial animal was invented by the Rishi (*Devabhaga,*[24] a son of *Sruta*). When he was departing from this life, he did not entrust (the secret to anyone). But a supernatural being communicated it to *Girija,* the son of *Babhru.* Since his time men study it.

What is said by the *Aitareya Brahmana* places two things beyond dispute. One is that the Brahmins monopolized the whole of the flesh of the sacrificial animal. Except for a paltry bit they did not even allow the sacrificer to share in it. The second is that the Brahmins themselves played the part of butchers in the slaughter of the animal. As a matter of principle the Brahmins should not eat the flesh of the animal killed at a sacrifice. The principle underlying yajna is that man should offer himself as sacrifice to the gods. He offers an animal only to release himself from this obligation. From this it followed that the animal, being only a substitute for the man, eating the flesh of animal meant eating human flesh.[25] This theory was very detrimental to the interest of the Brahmins who had a complete monopoly of the flesh of the animal offered for sacrifice. The *Aitareya Brahmana* which had seen in this theory the danger of the Brahmins being deprived of the flesh of the sacrificial animal takes pains to explain away the theory by a simple negation. It says:[26]

> The man who is initiated (into the sacrificial mysteries) offers himself to all deities. Agni represents all deities, and Soma represents all deities. When he (the sacrificer) offers the animal to *Agni-Soma* he releases himself (by being

represented by the animal) from being offered to all deities.

[...]

They say: 'do not eat from the animal offered to Agni-Soma.' 'Who eats from this animal, eats from human flesh; because the sacrificer releases himself (from being sacrificed) by means of the animal'. But this (precept) is not to be attended to.

Given these facts, no further evidence seems to be necessary to support the statement that the Brahmins were not merely beef-eaters but they were also butchers.

Why then did the Brahmins change front? Let us deal with their change of front in two stages. First, why did they give up beef-eating?

II

As has already been shown cow-killing was not legally prohibited by Asoka. Even if it had been prohibited, a law made by the Buddhist Emperor could never have been accepted by the Brahmins as binding upon them.

Did Manu prohibit beef-eating? If he did, then that would be binding on the Brahmins and would afford an adequate explanation of their change of front. Looking into the *Manusmriti* one does find the following verses:[27]

> V.46. He who does not seek to cause the sufferings of bonds and death to living creatures, (but) desires the good of all (beings), obtains endless bliss.
>
> V.47. He who does not injure any (creature), attains without an effort what he thinks of, what he undertakes, and what he fixes his mind on.
>
> V.48. Meat can never be obtained without injury to living

creatures, and injury to sentient beings is detrimental to (the attainment of) heavenly bliss; let him therefore shun (the use of) meat.

V.49. Having well considered the (disgusting) origin of flesh and the (cruelty of) fettering and slaying corporeal beings, let him entirely abstain from eating flesh.

If these verses can be treated as containing positive injunctions they would be sufficient to explain why the Brahmins gave up meat-eating and became vegetarians. But it is impossible to treat these verses as positive injunctions, carrying the force of law. They are either exhortations or interpolations introduced after the Brahmins had become vegetarians in praise of the change. That the latter is the correct view is proved by the following verses which occur in the same chapter of the *Manusmriti*:

V.28. The Lord of creatures (Prajapati)[28] created this whole (world to be) the sustenance of the vital spirit; both the immovable and the movable (creation is) the food of the vital spirit.

V.29. What is destitute of motion is the food of those endowed with locomotion; (animals) without fangs (are the food) of those with fangs, those without hands of those who possess hands, and the timid of the bold.

V.30. The eater who daily even devours those destined to be his food, commits no sin; for the creator himself created both the eaters and those who are to be eaten (for those special purposes).

V. 56. There is no sin in eating meat, in (drinking) spirituous liquor, and in carnal intercourse for that is the natural way of created beings, but abstention brings great rewards.

V. 27. One may eat meat when it has been sprinkled with water, while Mantras were recited, when Brahmanas desire (one's doing it) when one is engaged (in the performance of a rite) according to the law, and when one's life is in danger.

V. 31. 'The consumption of meat (is befitting) for sacrifices,' that is declared to be a rule made by the gods, but to persist (in using it) on other (occasions) is said to be a proceeding worthy of Rakshasas.

V. 32. He who eats meat, when he honours the gods and manes commits no sin, whether he has bought it, or himself has killed (the animal) or has received it as a present from others.

V. 42. A twice-born man who, knowing the true meaning of the Veda, slays an animal for these purposes, causes both himself and the animal to enter a most blessed state.

V. 39. Svayambhu (the Self-existent) himself created animals for the sake of sacrifices; sacrifices (have been instituted) for the good of this whole (world); hence the slaughtering (of beasts) for sacrifice is not slaughtering (in the ordinary sense of the word).

V. 40. Herbs, trees, cattle, birds, and (other) animals that have been destroyed for sacrifices, receive (being reborn) higher existences.

Manu goes further and makes eating of flesh compulsory. Note the following verse:

V. 35. But a man who, being duly engaged (to officiate or to dine at a sacred rite), refuses to eat meat, becomes after death an animal during twenty-one existences.

That Manu did not prohibit meat-eating is evident enough. That *Manusmriti* did not prohibit cow-killing can also be proved from the Smriti itself. In the first place, the only references to cow in the *Manusmriti* are to be found in the catalogue of rules which are made applicable by Manu to the Snataka.[29] They are set out below:

1. A Snataka should not eat food which a cow has smelt.[30]
2. A Snataka should not step over a rope to which a calf is tied.[31]
3. A Snataka should not urinate in a cow-pen.[32]
4. A Snataka should not answer the call of nature facing a cow.[33]
5. A Snataka should not keep his right arm uncovered when he enters a cow-pen.[34]
6. A Snataka should not interrupt a cow which is suckling her calf, nor tell anybody of it.[35]
7. A Snataka should not ride on the back of the cow.[36]
8. A Snataka should not offend the cow.[37]
9. A Snataka who is impure must not touch a cow with his hand.[38]

From these references it will be seen that Manu did not regard the cow as a sacred animal. On the other hand, he regarded it as an impure animal whose touch caused ceremonial pollution.[39]

There are verses in Manu which show that he did not prohibit the eating of beef. In this connection, reference may be made to Chapter III.3. It says:

> He (Snataka) who is famous (for the strict performance of) his duties and has received his heritage, the Veda from his father, shall be honoured, sitting on couch and adorned with a garland with (the present of) a cow (the honey-mixture).[40]

The question is why should Manu recommend the gift of a cow to a Snataka? Obviously, to enable him to perform Madhuparka. If that is so, it follows that Manu knew that Brahmins did eat beef and he had no objection to it.

Another reference would be to Manu's discussion of the animals whose meat is eatable and those whose meat is not. In Chapter V.18. he says:

The porcupine, the hedgehog, the iguana, the rhinoceros, the tortoise, and the hare they declare to be eatable: likewise those (domestic animals) that have teeth in one jaw only, excepting camels.[41]

In this verse Manu gives general permission to eat the flesh of all domestic animals that have teeth in one jaw only. To this rule Manu makes one exception, namely, the camel. In this class of domestic animals—those that have teeth in one jaw only—falls not only the camel but also the cow. It is noteworthy that Manu does not make an exception in the case of the cow. This means that Manu had no objection to the eating of the cow's flesh.

Manu did not make the killing of the cow an offence. Manu divides sins into two classes (i) mortal sins and (ii) minor sins.[42] Among the mortal sins Manu includes:

XI.55. Killing a Brahmana, drinking (the spirituous liquor called) Sura, stealing (the gold of Brahmana), adultery with a Guru's wife, and associating with such offenders they declare (to be) mortal sins (mahapataka).[43]

Among minor sins Manu includes:

XI.60. Killing the cow, sacrificing for those unworthy to sacrifice, adultery, selling oneself, casting off one's teacher, mother, father or son, giving up the (daily) study of the Veda and neglecting the (sacred domestic) fire.[44]

From this it will be clear that according to Manu cow-killing was only a minor sin.[45] It was reprehensible only if the cow was killed without good and sufficient reason. Even if it was otherwise, it was not heinous or inexplicable. The same was the attitude of Yajnavalkya.[46]

All this proves that for generations the Brahmins had been eating beef. Why did they give up beef-eating? Why did they, as an extreme step, give up meat eating altogether and become vegetarians? It is two revolutions rolled into one. As has been shown it has not been done as a result of the preachings of Manu, their Divine Law-maker. The revolution has taken place in spite of Manu and contrary to his directions. What made the Brahmins take this step? Was philosophy responsible for it? Or was it dictated by strategy? Two explanations are offered. One explanation is that this deification of the cow was a manifestation of the Advaita philosophy that one supreme entity pervaded the whole universe, that on that account all life human as well as animal was sacred. This explanation is obviously unsatisfactory. In the first place, it does not fit in with facts. The *Vedanta Sutra*[47] which proclaims the doctrine of oneness of life does not prohibit the killing of animals for sacrificial purposes as is evident from II.1.28.[48] In the second place, if the transformation was due to the desire to realize the ideal of Advaita then there is no reason why it should have stopped with the cow. It should have extended to all other animals.

Another explanation[49] more ingenious than the first, is that this transformation in the life of the Brahmin was due to the rise of the doctrine of the Transmigration of the Soul.[50] Even this explanation does not fit in with facts. The *Brahadaranyaka Upanishad*[51] upholds the doctrine of transmigration (VI.2)[52] and yet recommends that if a man desires to have a learned son born to him he should prepare a mass of the flesh of the bull or ox or of other flesh with rice and ghee. Again, how is it that this doctrine which is propounded in the Upanishads did not have any effect on the Brahmins up to the time of the *Manusmriti*, a period of at least 400 years. Obviously, this explanation is no explanation. Thirdly, if Brahmins became vegetarians by reason of the doctrine of transmigration of the soul how is it that it did not make the non-Brahmins take to vegetarianism?

To my mind, it was strategy which made the Brahmins give up beef-eating and start worshipping the cow. The clue to the worship of the cow is to be found in the struggle between Buddhism and Brahmanism and the means adopted by Brahmanism to establish its supremacy over Buddhism. The strife between Buddhism and Brahmanism is a crucial fact in Indian history. Without the realization of this fact, it is impossible to explain some of the features of Hinduism. Unfortunately students of Indian history have entirely missed the importance of this strife. They knew there was Brahmanism. But they seem to be entirely unaware of the struggle for supremacy in which these creeds were engaged and that their struggle which extended for 400 years has left some indelible marks on religion, society and politics of India.

This is not the place for describing the full story of the struggle. All one can do is to mention a few salient points. Buddhism was at one time the religion of the majority of the people of India. It continued to be the religion of the masses for hundreds of years. It attacked Brahmanism on all sides as no religion had done before.[53]

Brahmanism was on the wane and if not on the wane, it was certainly on the defensive. As a result of the spread of Buddhism, the Brahmins had lost all power and prestige at the Royal Court and among the people.[54] They were smarting under the defeat they had suffered at the hands of Buddhism and were making all possible efforts to regain their power and prestige. Buddhism had made so deep an impression on the minds of the masses and had taken such a hold of them that it was absolutely impossible for the Brahmins to fight the Buddhists except by accepting their ways and means and practising the Buddhist creed in its extreme form. After the death of Buddha his followers started setting up the images of the Buddha and building stupas. The Brahmins followed it.

They, in their turn, built temples and installed in them images of Shiva, Vishnu and Ram and Krishna etc.—all with the object of drawing away the crowd that was attracted by the image worship of Buddha.[55] That is how temples and images which had no place in Brahmanism came into Hinduism.[56] The Buddhists rejected the Brahmanic religion which consisted of yajna and animal sacrifice, particularly of the cow. The objection to the sacrifice of the cow had taken a strong hold of the minds of the masses especially as they were an agricultural population and the cow was a very useful animal. The Brahmins in all probability had come to be hated as the killer of cows in the same way as the guest had come to be hated as Goghna, the killer of the cow by the householder, because whenever he came a cow had to be killed in his honour. That being the case, the Brahmins could do nothing to improve their position against the Buddhists except by giving up the Yajna as a form of worship and the sacrifice of the cow.

That the object of the Brahmins in giving up beef-eating was to snatch away from the Buddhist Bhikshus the supremacy they had acquired is evidenced by the adoption of vegetarianism by Brahmins. Why did the Brahmins become vegetarian? The answer is that without becoming vegetarian the Brahmins could not have recovered the ground they had lost to their rival namely Buddhism. In this connection it must be remembered that there was one aspect in which Brahmanism suffered in public esteem as compared to Buddhism. That was the practice of animal sacrifice which was the essence of Brahmanism and to which Buddhism was deadly opposed. That in an agricultural population there should be respect for Buddhism and revulsion against Brahmanism which involved slaughter of animals including cows and bullocks is only natural.[57] What could the Brahmins do to recover the lost ground? To go one better than the Buddhist Bhikshus not only to give up meat-eating but to become vegetarians—which they did. That this was the object of the Brahmins in becoming vegetarians can be proved in various ways.[58]

If the Brahmins had acted from conviction that animal sacrifice was bad, all that was necessary for them to do was to give up killing animals for sacrifice. It was unnecessary for them to be vegetarians. That they did go in for vegetarianism makes it obvious that their motive was far-reaching. Secondly, it was unnecessary for them to become vegetarians. For the Buddhist Bhikshus were not vegetarians. This statement might surprise many people owing to the popular belief that the connection between Ahimsa and Buddhism was immediate and essential. It is generally believed that the Buddhist Bhikshus eschewed animal food [meat]. This is an error. The fact is that the Buddhist Bhikshus were permitted to eat three kinds of flesh that were deemed pure. Later on they were extended to five classes. Yuan Chwang,[59] the Chinese traveller was aware of this and spoke of the pure kinds of flesh as *San-Ching*. The origin of this practice among the Bhikshus is explained by Mr Thomas Watters.[60]

According to the story told by him[61]—

> In the time of Buddha there was in Vaisali[62] a wealthy general named Siha who was a convert to Buddhism. He became a liberal supporter of the Brethren and kept them constantly supplied with good flesh-food. When it was noticed abroad that the Bhikshus were in the habit of eating such food specially provided for them, the Tirthikas made the practice a matter of angry reproach. Then the abstemious ascetic Brethren, learning this, reported the circumstances to the Master, who thereupon called the Brethren together. When they assembled, he announced to them the law that

> they were not to eat the flesh of any animal which they had seen put to death for them, or about which they had been told that it had been slain for them. But he permitted to the Brethern as 'pure' (that is, lawful) food the flesh of animals the slaughter of which had not been seen by the Bhikshus, not heard of by them, and not suspected by them to have been on their account. In the Pali and *Ssu*-fen[63] Vinaya it was after a breakfast given by Siha to the Buddha and some of the Brethren, for which the carcass of a large ox was procured that the Nirgranthas reviled the Bhikshus and Buddha instituted this new rule declaring fish and flesh 'pure' in the three conditions. The animal food now permitted to the Bhikshus came to be known as the 'three pures' or 'three pure kinds of flesh', and it was tersely described as 'unseen, unheard, unsuspected', or as the Chinese translations sometimes have it 'not seen, not heard nor suspected to be on my account'. Then two more kinds of animal food were declared lawful for the Brethren viz., the flesh of animals which had died a natural death, and that of animals which had been killed by a bird of prey or other savage creature. So there came to be five classes or descriptions of flesh which the professed Buddhist was at liberty to use as food. Then the 'unseen, unheard, unsuspected' came to be treated as one class, and this together with the 'natural death' and 'bird killed' made a *san-ching.*

As the Buddhist Bhikshus did eat meat the Brahmins had no reason to give it up. Why then did the Brahmins give up meat-eating and become vegetarians? It was because they did not want to put themselves merely on the same footing in the eyes of the public as the Buddhist Bhikshus.

The giving up of the yajna system and abandonment of the sacrifice of the cow could have had only a limited effect. At the most it would have put the Brahmins on the same footing as the Buddhists. The same would have been the case if they had followed the rules observed by the Buddhist Bhikshus in the matter of meat-eating. It could not have given the Brahmins the means of achieving supremacy over the Buddhists which was their ambition. They wanted to oust the Buddhists from the place of honour and respect which they had acquired in the minds of the masses by their opposition to the killing of the cow for sacrificial purposes. To achieve their purpose the Brahmins had to adopt the usual tactics of a reckless adventurer. It is to beat extremism by extremism. It is the strategy which all rightists use to overcome the leftists. The only way to beat the Buddhists was to go a step further and be vegetarians.[64]

There is another reason which can be relied upon to support the thesis that the Brahmins started cow-worship, gave up beef-eating and became vegetarians in order to vanquish Buddhism. It is the date when cow-killing became a mortal sin. It is well known that cow-killing was not made an offence by Asoka. Many people expect him to have come forward to prohibit the killing of the cow. Prof Vincent Smith regards it as surprising.[65] But there is nothing surprising in it.

Buddhism was against animal sacrifice in general. It had no particular affection for the cow. Asoka had therefore no particular reason to make a law to save the cow. What is more astonishing is the fact that cow-killing was made a Mahapataka,[66] a mortal sin or a capital offence by the Gupta Kings[67] who were champions of Hinduism which recognized and sanctioned the killing of the cow for sacrificial purposes. As pointed out by Mr D.R. Bhandarkar[68]—

> We have got the incontrovertible evidence of inscriptions to show that early in the 5th century AD killing a cow was looked upon as an offence of the deepest turpitude,

turpitude as deep as that involved in murdering a Brahman. We have thus a copper-plate inscription dated 465 AD and referring itself to the reign of Skandagupta of the Imperial Gupta dynasty. It registers a grant and ends with a verse saying: 'Whosoever will transgress this grant that has been assigned (shall become as guilty as) the slayer of a cow, the slayer of a spiritual preceptor (or) the slayer of a Brahman. A still earlier record placing *go-hatya* on the same footing as *brahma hatya* is that of Chandragupta II, grandfather of Skandagupta just mentioned. It bears the Gupta date 93, which is equivalent to 412 AD. It is engraved on the railing which surrounds the celebrated Buddhist stupa at Sanchi, in Central India. This also speaks of a benefaction made by an officer of Chandragupta and ends as follows: ... "Whosoever shall interfere with this arrangement ... he shall become invested with (the guilt of) the slaughter of a cow or of a Brahman, and with (the guilt of) the five *anantarya*." Here the object of this statement is to threaten the resumer of the grant, be he a Brahminist or a Buddhist, with the sins regarded as mortal by each community. The *anantaryas* are the five *mahapatakas* according to Buddhist theology. They are: matricide, patricide, killing an Arhant,[69] shedding the blood of a Buddha, and causing a split among the priesthood. The *mahapatakas* with which a Brahminist is here threatened are only two: viz., the killing of a cow and the murdering of a Brahman. The latter is obviously a *mahapataka* as it is mentioned as such in all the Smritis, but the former has been specified only [as] an upapataka by Apastamba, Manu, Yajnavalkya and so forth. But the very fact that it is here associated with *brahma-hatya* and both have been put on a par with the *anantaryas* of the Buddhists shows that in the beginning of the fifth century AD, it was raised to the

> category of *mahapatakas*. Thus *go-hatya* must have come to be considered a *mahapataka* at least one century earlier, i.e., about the commencement of the fourth century AD.

The question is why should a Hindu king have come forward to make a law against cow-killing, that is to say, against the Laws of Manu? The answer is that the Brahmins had to suspend or abrogate a requirement of their Vedic religion in order to overcome the supremacy of the Buddhist Bhikshus. If the analysis is correct then it is obvious that the worship of the cow is the result of the struggle between Buddhism and Brahminism. It was a means adopted by the Brahmins to regain their lost position.

Chapter XIV
Why should beef-eating make Broken Men Untouchables?

The stoppage of beef-eating by the Brahmins and the non-Brahmins and the continued use thereof by the Broken Men had produced a situation which was different from the old. This difference lay in the fact that while in the old situation everybody ate beef, in the new situation one section did not and another did. The difference was a glaring difference. Everybody could see it. It divided society as nothing else did before. All the same, this difference need not have given rise to such extreme division of society as is marked by Untouchability. It could have remained a social difference. There are many cases where different sections of the community differ in their foods. What one likes the other dislikes and yet this difference does not create a bar between the two.

There must therefore be some special reason why in India the difference between the Settled Community and the Broken Men in the matter of beef-eating created a bar between the two. What can that be? The answer is that if beef-eating had remained a secular affair—a mere matter of individual taste—such a bar between those who ate beef and those who did not wouldn't have arisen. Unfortunately beef-eating, instead of being treated as a purely secular matter, was made a matter of religion. This happened because the Brahmins made the cow a sacred animal. This made beef-eating a sacrilege. The Broken Men being guilty of sacrilege necessarily became beyond the pale of society.

The answer may not be quite clear to those who have no idea of the scope and function of religion in the life of the society. They may ask: Why should religion make such a difference? It will be clear if the following points regarding the scope and function of religion are borne in mind.

To begin with the definition[1] of religion. There is one universal feature which characterizes all religions. This feature lies in religion being a unified system of beliefs and practices which (1) relate to sacred things and (2) which unite into one single community all those who adhere to them. To put it slightly differently, there are two elements in every religion. One is that religion is inseparable from sacred things. The other is that religion is a collective thing inseparable from society.

> The first element in religion presupposes a classification of all things, real and ideal, which are the subject matter of man's thought, into two distinct classes which are generally designated by two distinct terms the *sacred* and the *profane,* popularly spoken of as secular.

This defines the scope of religion. For understanding the function of religion the following points regarding things sacred should be noted:

The first thing to note is that things sacred are not merely higher than or superior in dignity and status to those that are profane. They are just different. The sacred and the profane do not belong to the same class. There is a complete dichotomy between the two. As Prof Durkheim observes:[2] The traditional opposition of good and bad is nothing beside this; for the good and the bad are only two opposed species of the same class, namely, morals, just as sickness and health are two different aspects of the same order of facts, life, while the sacred and the profane have always and everywhere been conceived by the human mind as two distinct classes, as two worlds between which there is nothing in common.[3]

The curious may want to know what has led men to see in this world this dichotomy between the sacred and the profane. We must however refuse to enter into this discussion as it is unnecessary for the immediate purpose we have in mind.[4]

Confining ourselves to the issue the next thing to note is that the circle of sacred objects is not fixed. Its extent varies infinitely from religion to religion. Gods and spirits are not the only sacred things. A rock, a tree, an animal, a spring, a pebble, a piece of wood, a house, in a word anything can be sacred.

Things sacred are always associated with interdictions otherwise called *taboos.* To quote Prof. Durkheim again:[5]

> Sacred things are those which the interdictions protect and isolate; profane things, those to which these interdictions are applied and which must remain at a distance from the first.

Religious interdicts take multiple forms.[6] Most important of these is the interdiction on contact. The interdiction on contact rests upon the principle that the profane should never touch the sacred. Contact may be established in a variety of ways other than touch. A look is a means of contact. That is why the sight of sacred things is forbidden to the profane in certain cases. For instance, women are not allowed to see certain things which are regarded as sacred. The word (i.e., the breath which forms part of man and which spreads outside him) is another means of contact. That is why the profane is forbidden to address the sacred things or to utter them. For instance, the Veda must be uttered only by the Brahmin and not by the Shudra. An exceptionally intimate contact is the one resulting from the absorption of food. Hence comes the interdiction against eating the sacred animals or vegetables.

The interdictions relating to the sacred are not open to discussion. They are beyond discussion and must be accepted without question. The sacred is 'untouchable' in the sense that it is beyond the pale of debate. All that one can do is to respect and obey.

Lastly the interdictions relating to the sacred are binding on all. They are not maxims. They are injunctions. They are obligatory but not in the ordinary sense of the word. They partake of the nature of a categorical imperative.[7] Their breach is more than a crime. It is a sacrilege.

The above summary should be enough for an understanding of the scope and function of religion. It is unnecessary to enlarge upon the subject further. The analysis of the working of the laws of the sacred which is the core of religion should enable any one to see that my answer to the question why beef-eating should make the Broken Men Untouchable is the correct one. All that is necessary to reach the answer I have proposed is to read the analysis of the working of the laws of the sacred with the cow as the sacred object. It will be found that Untouchability is the result of the breach of the interdiction against the eating of the sacred animal, namely, the cow.

As has been said, the Brahmins made the cow a sacred animal. They did not stop to make a difference between a living cow and a dead cow. The cow was sacred, living or dead. Beef-eating was not merely a crime. If it was only a crime it would have involved nothing more than punishment. Beef-eating was made a sacrilege. Anyone who treated the cow as profane was guilty of sin and unfit for association.[8] The Broken Men who continued to eat beef became guilty of sacrilege.

Once the cow became sacred and the Broken Men continued to eat beef, there was no other fate left for the Broken Men except to be treated [as] unfit for association, i.e., as Untouchables.

Before closing the subject it may be desirable to dispose of possible objections to the thesis. Two such objections to the thesis appear obvious. One is what evidence is there that the Broken Men did eat the flesh of the dead cow. The second is why they did not give up beef-eating when the Brahmins and the non-Brahmins abandoned it. These questions have an important bearing upon the theory of the origin of Untouchability advanced in this book and must therefore be dealt with.

The first question is relevant as well as crucial. If the Broken Men were eating beef from the very beginning, then obviously the theory cannot stand. For, if they were eating beef from the very beginning and nonetheless were not treated as Untouchables, to say that the Broken Men became Untouchables because of beef-eating would be illogical if not senseless. The second question is relevant, if not crucial. If the Brahmins gave up beef-eating and the non-Brahmins imitated them why did the Broken Men not do the same? If the law made the killing of the cow a capital sin because the cow became a sacred animal to the Brahmins and non-Brahmins, why were the Broken Men not stopped from eating beef? If they had been stopped from eating beef there would have been no Untouchability.

The answer to the first question is that even during the period when beef-eating was common to both, the Settled Tribesmen and the Broken Men, a system had grown up whereby the Settled Community ate fresh beef, while the Broken Men ate the flesh of the dead cow. We have no positive evidence to show that members of the Settled Community never ate the flesh of the dead cow. But we have negative evidence which shows that the dead cow had become an exclusive possession and perquisite of the Broken Men. The evidence consists of facts which relate to the Mahars[9] of Maharashtra to whom reference has already been made. As has already been pointed out, the Mahars of Maharashtra claim the right to take the dead animal. This right they claim against every Hindu in the village. This means that no Hindu can eat the flesh of his own animal when it dies. He has to surrender it to the Mahar. This is merely another way of stating that when eating beef was a common practice the Mahars ate dead beef and the Hindus ate fresh beef. The only questions that arise are: Whether what is true of the present is true of the ancient past? Can this fact which is true of Maharashtra be taken as typical of the arrangement between the Settled Tribes and the Broken Men throughout India?

In this connection reference may be made to the tradition current among the Mahars according to which they claim that they were given 52 rights[10] against the Hindu villagers by the Muslim king of Bedar. Assuming that they were given by the king of Bedar, the King obviously did not create them for the first time. They must have been in existence from the ancient past. What the king did was merely to confirm them. This means that the practice of the Broken Men eating dead meat and the Settled Tribes eating fresh meat must have grown in the ancient past. That such an arrangement should grow up is certainly most natural. The Settled Community was a wealthy community with agriculture and cattle as means of livelihood. The Broken Men were a community of paupers with no means of livelihood and entirely dependent upon the Settled Community. The principal item of food for both was beef. It was possible for the Settled Community to kill an animal for food because it was possessed of cattle. The Broken Men could not for they had none. Would it be unnatural in these circumstances for the Settled Community to have agreed to give to the Broken Men its dead animals as part of their wages of watch and ward? Surely not. It can therefore be taken for granted that in the ancient past when both the Settled Community and Broken Men did eat beef the former ate fresh beef and the latter of the dead cow and that this system represented a universal state of affairs throughout India and was not confined to Maharashtra alone.

This disposes of the first objection. To turn to the second objection. The law made by the Gupta Emperors[11] was intended to prevent those who killed cows. It did not apply to the Broken Men. For they did not kill the cow. They only ate the dead cow. Their conduct did not contravene the law against cow-killing. The practice of eating the flesh of the dead cow therefore was allowed to continue. Nor did their conduct contravene the doctrine of Ahimsa assuming that it has anything to do with the abandonment of beef-eating by the Brahmins and the non-Brahmins. Killing the cow was Himsa. But eating the dead cow was not. The Broken Men had therefore no cause for feeling qualms of conscience in continuing to eat the dead cow. Neither the law nor the doctrine of Himsa could interdict what they were doing, for what they were doing was neither contrary to law nor to the doctrine.

As to why they did not imitate the Brahmins and the non-Brahmins the answer is two-fold. In the first place, imitation[12] was too costly. They could not afford it. The flesh of the dead cow was their principal sustenance. Without it they would starve. In the second place, carrying the dead cow had become an obligation[13] though originally it was a privilege. As they could not escape carrying the dead cow they did not mind using the flesh as food in the manner in which they were doing previously.

The objections therefore do not invalidate the thesis in any way.

Part VI

UNTOUCHABILITY AND THE DATE OF ITS BIRTH

Chapter XV
The Impure and the Untouchables

I

When did Untouchability come into existence? The orthodox Hindus insist that it is very ancient in its origin. In support of their contention reliance is placed on the fact that the observance of Untouchability is enjoined not merely by the Smritis which are of a later date but it is also enjoined by the Dharma Sutras which are much earlier and which, according to certain authors, date some centuries before Christ.[1]

In a study devoted to exploring the origin of Untouchability the question one must begin with is: Is Untouchability as old as is suggested to be?

For an answer to this question one has to examine the Dharma Sutras in order to ascertain what they mean when they refer to Untouchability and to the Untouchables. Do they mean by Untouchability what we understand by it today? Do [Are] the class, to which they refer, Untouchables in the sense in which we use the term Untouchables today?

To begin with the first question. An examination of the Dharma Sutras no doubt shows that they speak of a class whom they call Asprashya. There is also no doubt that the term Asprashya does mean Untouchables. The question however remains whether the Asprashya of the Dharma Sutras are the same as the Asprashya of modern India. This question becomes important when it is realized that the Dharma Sutras also use a variety of other terms such as Antya,

Antyaja, Antyavasin and Bahya. These terms are also used by the later Smritis. It might do us well to have some idea of the use of these terms by the different Sutras and Smritis. The following table is intended to serve that purpose:[2]

I. Asprashya

Dharma Sutra	Smriti
1. Vishnu V.104	1. Katyayana verses 433, 783

II. Antya

Dharma Sutra	Smriti
1. Vasishta. (16.30)	1. Manu IV.79; VIII. 68
2. Apastambha (III.I)[3]	2. Yajnavalkya I.148, 197
	3. Atri 25.4; Likhita 92[4]

III. Bahya

Dharma Sutra	Smriti
1. Apastambha 1.2.39.18[5]	Manu 28[6]
2. Vishnu 16.14	Narada I.155[7]

IV. Antyavasin

Dharma Sutra	Smriti
1. Gautama XXXI; XXIII 32[8]	1. Manu IV.79; X.39
2. Vasishta XVIII. 3	2. Shanti Parva, Mahabharata 141: 29–32
	3. Madhyamangiras (quoted in Mitakshara on Yaj. 3.280)[9]

V. Antyaja

Dharma Sutra	Smriti
1. Vishnu 36.7	1. Manu IV.61; VIII.279 2. Yajnavalkya 1.273 3. Brihadyanya Smriti (quoted by Mitakshara on Yajnavalkya III. 260)[10] 4. Atri. 1995. Veda Vyas I.12–13[11]

The next question is whether the classes indicated by the terms Antya, Antyaja, Antyavasin and Bahya are the same as those indicated by the term Asprashya which etymologically means an Untouchable. In other words are they only different names for the same class of people?

It is an unfortunate fact that the Dharma Sutras do not enable us to answer this question. The term *Asprashya* occurs in two places (once in one Sutra and twice in one Smriti). But not one gives an enumeration of the classes included in it. The same is the case with the term *Antya*. Although the word *Antya* occurs in six places (in two Sutras and four Smritis) not one enumerates who they are. Similarly, the word *Bahya* occurs in four places (in two Sutras and two Smritis), but none of them mentions what communities are included under this term. The only exception is with regard to the terms Antyavasin and Antyajas. Here again no Dharma Sutra enumerates them. But there is an enumeration of them in the Smritis.[12] The enumeration of the Antyavasin occurs in the Smriti known as *Madhyamangiras* and that of the Antyajas in the *Atri Smriti* and *Veda Vyas Smriti*. Who they are, will be apparent from the following table:

ANTYAVASIN	ANTYAJA	
Madhyamangiras	Atri	Veda Vyas
1. Chandala	1. Nata	1. Chandala
2. Shvapaka	2. Meda	2. Shvapaka
3. Kshatta	3. Bhilla	3. Nata
4. Suta	4. Rajaka	4. Meda
5. Vaidehika	5. Charmakar	5. Bhilla
6. Magadha	6. Buruda	6. Rajaka
7. Ayogava	7. Kayavarta	7. Charmakar
		8. Virat
		9. Dasa
		10. Bhatt
		11. Kolika
		12.Pushkar

From this table it is quite clear that there is neither precision nor agreement with regard to the use of the terms Antyavasin and Antyaja. For instance Chandala and Shvapaka fall in both the categories Antyavasin and Antyaja according to *Madhyamangiras* and *Veda Vyas*. But when one compares *Madhyamangiras* with *Atri* they fall in different categories. The same is true with regard to the term Antyaja. For example while (1) Chandala and (2) Shvapaka are Antyajas according to *Veda Vyas*, according to *Atri* they are not. Again according to *Atri* (1) Buruda and (2) Kayavarta are Antyajas while according to *Veda Vyas* they are not. Again (1) Virat (2) Dasa (3) Bhatt (4) Kolika and (5) Pushkar are Antyaja according to *Veda Vyas* but according to *Atri* they are not.

To sum up the position reached so far: neither the Dharma Sutras nor the Smritis help us to ascertain who were included in the category of Asprashya. Equally useless are the Dharma Sutras and the Smritis to enable us to ascertain whether the classes spoken of as Antyavasin, Antyaja and Bahya were the same as Asprashya. Is there any other way of ascertaining whether any of these formed into the category of Asprashya or Untouchables? It would be better to collect together whatever information is available about each of these classes.[13]

What about the Bahyas? Who are they? What are they? Are they Untouchables? They are mentioned by Manu. To understand their position, it is necessary to refer to Manu's scheme of social classification. Manu divides the people into various categories. He first[14] makes a broad division between (1) Vaidikas and (2) Dasyus. He then proceeds to divide the Vaidikas into four sub-divisions: (1) Those inside Chaturvarnya (2) Those outside Chaturvarnya (3) Vratya and (4) Patitas or outcastes.

Whether a person was inside Chaturvarnya or outside, was a question to be determined by the Varna of the parents. If he was born of the parents of the same Varnas, he was inside the Chaturvarnya. If, on the other hand, he was born of parents of different Varnas i.e., he was the progeny of mixed marriages or what Manu calls *Varna Samkara,* then he was outside the Chaturvarnya. Those outside Chaturvarnya are further sub-divided by Manu into two classes. (1) Anulomas and (2) Pratilomas. Anulomas[15] were those whose fathers were of a higher Varna and mothers of a lower Varna. Pratilomas, on the other hand, were those whose fathers were of a lower Varna and the mothers of a higher Varna. Though both the Anulomas and Pratilomas were alike for the reason that they were outside the Chaturvarnya, Manu proceeds to make a distinction between them. The Anulomas, he calls *Varna Bahya* or shortly *Bahyas*, while Pratilomas he calls *Hinas.*[16] The Hinas are lower than the Bahyas. But neither the Bahyas nor the Hinas does Manu regard as Untouchables.

Antya as a class is mentioned in Manu IV.79.[17] Manu however does not enumerate them. Medhatithi[18] in his commentary suggests that Antya means Mleccha, such as Meda, etc.[19] Bühler translates Antya as a low-caste man.[20]

There is thus nothing to indicate that the Antyas were Untouchables. In all probability, it is the name given to those people who were living in the outskirts or *end* (Anta) of the village. The reason why they came to be regarded as low is to be found in the story narrated in the *Brahadaranyaka Upanishad* (1.3) to which reference is made by Mr Kane.[21] The story is that:

> Gods and Asuras had a strife and the Gods thought that they might rise superior to the Asuras by the Udgitha. In this vidya occurs the passage, 'this devata (Prana) throwing aside the sin that was death to these devatas (vak, etc.) sent it to ends of these devatas there; therefore one should not go to the people (outside the Aryan pale) nor to the ends [*disam anta*] (of the quarters) thinking, otherwise I may fall in with *papman* i.e., death.

The meaning of Antya turns on the connotation of the phrase 'disam anta' which occurs in the passage quoted above. If the phrase 'ends of the quarters' can be translated as meaning the end of the periphery of the village, without its being called a far-fetched translation, we have here an explanation of what Antya originally meant. It does not suggest that the Antyas were Untouchables. It only meant that they were living on the outskirts of the village.

As to the Antyajas, what we know about them is enough to refute the view that they were Untouchables. Attention may be drawn to the following facts:[22]

In the Shanti Parvan (109.19) of the Mahabharata there is a reference to Antyajas who are spoken of as soldiers in the army. According to *Sarasvativilasa*,[23] Pitamaha speaks of the seven cases of Rajakas included in the term Antyaja as Prakritis. That Prakritis mean trade guilds such as of washermen and others is quite clear from the Sangamner Plate of Bhillama II dated Saka 922[24] which records the grant of a village to eighteen Prakritis. *Viramitrodaya*[25] says that Srenis mean the eighteen castes such as the Rajaka, etc., which are collectively called Antyajas. In view of these facts how could the Antyajas be said to have been regarded as the Untouchables?

Coming to the Antyavasin, who were they? Were they Untouchables? The term Antyavasin has been used in two different senses. In one sense it was applied to a Brahmachari living in the house of the guru during his term of studentship. A Brahmachari was referred to as Antyavasin.[26] It probably meant one who was served last. Whatever the reason for calling a Brahmachari Antyavasin it is beyond dispute that the word in that connection could not connote Untouchability. How could it when only Brahmins, Kshatriyas and Vaishyas could become Brahmacharis. In another sense they refer to a body of people. But even in this sense it is doubtful if it means Untouchables.

According to Vas.Dh.Sutra (18.3)[27] they are the offspring of a Sudra father and Vaishya mother. But according to Manu (V.39)[28] they are the offspring of a Chandala father and a Nishad mother. As to the class to which they belong, the *Mitakshara* says they are a sub-group of the Antyajas which means that the Antyavasin were not different from the Antyajas. What is therefore true of the Antyajas may also be taken as true of the Antyavasin.

III

Stopping here to take stock of the situation as it emerges from such information as we have regarding the social condition of the people called Antyavasin, Antya, Antyaja, as is available from ancient literature, obviously it is not open to say that these classes were Untouchables in the modern sense of the term.

However, for the satisfaction of those who may still have some doubt, the matter may be further examined from another point of view. Granting that they were described as Asprashya, we may proceed to inquire as to what was the connotation of the term in the days of the Dharma Sutras.

For this purpose we must ascertain the rules of atonement prescribed by the Shastras. From the study of these rules we will be able to see whether the term Asprashya had the same connotation in the times of the Dharma Sutras as it has now.

Let us take the case of the Chandalas as an illustration of the class called Asprashya. In the first place, it should be remembered that the word Chandala does not denote one single homogenous class of people. It is one word for many classes of people, all different from one another. There are altogether five different classes of Chandalas who are referred to in the Shastras. They are (i) the offspring of a Shudra father and a Brahmin mother,[29] (ii) the offspring of an unmarried woman,[30] (iii) the offspring of union with a sagotra woman,[31] (iv) the offspring of a person who after becoming an ascetic turns back to the householder's life[32] and (v) the offspring of a barber father and a Brahmin mother.[33]

It is difficult to say which Chandala calls for purification. We shall assume that purification is necessary in the case of all the Chandalas. What is the rule of purification prescribed by the Shastras?

Gautama in his Dharma Sutra (Chapter XIV, Verse 30)[34] also refers to it in the following terms:

> On touching an outcaste, a Chandala, a woman impure on

account of her confinement, a woman in her courses, or a corpse and on touching persons who have touched them, he shall purify himself by bathing dressed in his clothes.

Below is the text of the rule given by the *Vasistha Dharma Sutra* (Chapter IV, Verse 37):[35]

> When he has touched a sacrificial post, a pyre, a burial ground, a menstruating or a lately confined woman, impure men or Chandalas and so forth, he shall bathe, submerging both his body and his head.

Baudhayana agrees with Vasistha for he too in his Dharma Sutra (Prasna 1, Adhyaya 5, Khanda 6, Verse 5) says:

> On touching a tree standing on a sacred spot, a funeral pyre, a sacrificial post, a Chandala or a person who sells the Veda, a Brahmin shall bathe dressed in his clothes.[36]

The following are the rules contained in Manu:[37]

> V.85: When he (the Brahmin) has touched a Chandala, a menstruating woman, an outcaste, a woman in childbed, a corpse, or one who has touched a (corpse), he becomes pure by bathing.
>
> V.131: Manu has declared that the flesh of an animal killed by dogs is pure, likewise (that) of a (beast) slain by carnivorous (animals) or by men of low caste (Dasya) such as Chandalas.
>
> V.143: He who, while carrying anything in any manner, is touched by an impure (person or thing), shall become pure, if he performs an ablution, without pulling down that object.

From these texts drawn from the Dharma Sutras as well as Manu, the following points are clear:

(1) That the pollution by the touch of the Chandala was observed by the Brahmin only.

(2) That the pollution was probably observed on ceremonial occasions only.

IV

If these conclusions are right then this is a case of Impurity as distinguished from Untouchability. The distinction between the Impure and the Untouchable is very clear. The Untouchable pollutes all while the Impure pollutes only the Brahmin. The touch of the Impure causes pollution only on a ceremonial occasion. The touch of the Untouchable causes pollution at all times.

There is another argument to which so far no reference has been made which completely disproves the theory that the communities mentioned in the Dharma Sutras were Untouchables. That argument emerges out of a comparison of the list of communities given in the Order-in-Council (which is reproduced in Chapter II) with the list given in this chapter prepared from the Smritis.[38] What does the comparison show? As anyone can see, it shows:

Firstly: The maximum number of communities mentioned in the *Smritis* is only twelve, while the number of communities mentioned in the Order-in-Council comes to 429.

Secondly: There are communities which find a place in the Order-in-Council but which do not find a place in the *Smritis*. Out of the total of 429 there are nearly 426 which are unknown to the *Smritis*.

Thirdly: There are communities mentioned in the *Smritis* which do not find a place in the Order-in-Council at all.

Fourthly: There is only one community which finds a place in both. It is the Charmakar community.

Those who do not admit that the Impure are different from the Untouchables do not seem to be aware of these facts. But they will have to reckon with them. These facts are so significant and so telling that they cannot but force the conclusion that the two are different.

1. Out of the 429 communities mentioned in the Order-in-Council, there are only three which are to be found in the list given by the Smritis.
2. There are also two other communities mentioned in both lists (1) Nata and (2) Rajaka. But according to the Order-in-Council they are Untouchables in some parts of the country only. The Chamar is Untouchable throughout India.

Take the first fact. It raises a very important question.

If the two lists refer to one and the same class of people, why do they differ, and differ so widely? How is it that the communities mentioned in the Shastras do not appear in the list given in the Order-in-Council? Contrarywise, how is it that the communities mentioned in the Order-in-Council are not to be found in the list given by the Shastras? This is the first difficulty we have to face.

On the assumption that they refer to the same class of people, the question, assumes a serious character. If they refer to the same class of people then obviously Untouchability which was originally confined to twelve communities came to be extended to 429 communities! What has led to this vast extension of the Empire of Untouchability? If these 429 communities belong to the same class as the twelve mentioned by the Shastras why none of the Shastras mention them? It cannot be that none of the 429 communities were not in existence at the time when the Shastras were written. If all of them were not in existence at least some of them must have been. Why even such as did exist find no mention?

On the footing that both the lists belong to the same class of people, it is difficult to give any satisfactory answer to these questions. If, on the other hand, it is assumed that these lists refer to two different classes of people, all these questions disappear. The two lists are different because the list contained in the Shastras is a list of the Impure and the list contained in the Order-in-Council is a list of the Untouchables. This is the reason why the two lists differ. The divergence in the two lists merely emphasizes what has been urged on other grounds, namely, that the classes mentioned in Shastras are only Impure and it is a mistake to confound them with the Untouchables of the present day.

Now, turn to the second. If the Impure are the same as the Untouchables, why is it as many as 427 out of 429 should be unknown to the Smritis? As communities, they must have been in existence at the time of the Smritis. If they are Untouchables now, they must have been Untouchables then. Why then did the Smritis fail to mention them?

What about the third? If the Impure and the Untouchables are one and the same, why those communities which find a place in the Smritis do not find a place in the list given in the Order-in-Council? There are only two answers to this question. One is that though Untouchables at one time, they ceased to be Untouchables subsequently. The other is that the two lists contain names of communities who fall in altogether different categories. The first answer is untenable. For, Untouchability is permanent. Time cannot erase it or cleanse it. The only possible conclusion is the second.

Take the fourth. Why should Chamar alone find a place in the lists? The answer is not that the two lists include the same class of people. If it was the true answer, then not only the Chamar but all others included in the list given by the Smritis should appear in both the lists. But they do not. The true answer is that the two lists contain two different classes of people. The reason why some of those in the list of the Impure appear in the list of the Untouchables is that the Impure at one time became Untouchables. That the Chamar appears in both is far from being evidence to support the view that there is no difference between the Impure and the Untouchables. It proves that the Chamar who was at one time an Impure, subsequently became an Untouchable and had therefore to be included in both the lists. Of the twelve communities mentioned in the Smritis as Impure communities, only the Chamar should have been degraded to the status of an Untouchable is not difficult to explain. What has made the difference between the Chamar and the other impure communities is the fact of beef-eating. It is only those among the Impure who were eating beef that became Untouchables, when the cow became sacred and beef-eating became a sin. The Chamar is the only beef-eating community. That is why it alone appears in both the lists. The answer to the question relating to the Chamars is decisive on two points. It is conclusive on the point that the Impure are different from the Untouchables. It is also decisive on the point that it is beef-eating which is the root of Untouchability and which divides the Impure and the Untouchables.

The conclusion that Untouchability is not the same as Impurity has an important bearing on the determination of the date of birth of Untouchability. Without it any attempt at fixing the date would be missing the mark.

Chapter XVI
When did Broken Men become Untouchables?

The foregoing researches and discussions have proved that there was a time when the village in India consisted of a Settled Community and Broken Men and that though both lived apart, the former inside the village and the latter outside it, there was no bar to social intercourse between the members of the Settled Community and the Broken Men. When the cow became sacred and beef-eating became taboo, society became divided into two—the Settled Community became a touchable community and Broken Men became an untouchable community. When did the Broken Men come to be regarded as Untouchables? That is the last question that remains to be considered. There are obvious difficulties in the way of fixing a precise date for the birth of Untouchability. Untouchability is an aspect of social psychology. It is a sort of social nausea of one group against another group. Being an outgrowth of social psychology which must have taken some time to acquire form and shape, nobody can venture to fix a precise date to a phenomenon which probably began as a cloud no bigger than man's hand and grew till it took its final all-pervading shape as we know it today. When could the seed of Untouchability be said to have been sown? If it is not possible to fix an exact date, is it possible to fix an approximate date?

An exact date is not possible. But it is possible to give an approximate date. For this the first thing to do is to begin by fixing the upper time-limit at which Untouchability did not exist and the lower time-limit at which it had come into operation.

To begin with the question of fixing the upper limit the first thing to note is that those who are called Antyajas are mentioned in the Vedas. But they were not only not regarded as Untouchables but they were not even regarded as Impure. The following extract from Kane may be quoted in support of this conclusion. Says Kane:[1]

> In the early Vedic literature several of the names of castes that are spoken of in the Smritis as Antyajas occur. We have Carmamna (a tanner of hides) in the Rig Veda (VIII.5.38),[2] the Chandala and Paulkasa occur in Vaj. S., the Vapa or Vapta[3] (barber) even in the Rig., the Vidalakara or Bidalakar[4] (corresponding to the Buruda[5] of the Smritis) occurs in the Vaj.S. and the Tai.Br. Vasahpalpuli[6] (washer woman) corresponding to the Rajakas[7] of the Smritis in Vaj.S. But there is no indication in these passages whether they, even if they formed castes, were at all Untouchables.

Thus in Vedic times there was no Untouchability. As to the period of the Dharma Sutras, we have seen that there was Impurity but there was no Untouchability.

Was there Untouchability in the time of Manu? This question cannot be answered offhand. There is a passage[8] in which he says that there are only four varnas and that there is no fifth varna. The passage is enigmatic. It is difficult to make out what it means. Quite obviously the statement by Manu is an attempt to settle a controversy that must have been going on at the time he wrote. Quite obviously the controversy was about the status of a certain class in relation to the system of Chaturvarna. Equally obvious is the point which was the centre of the controversy. To put briefly, the point was whether this class was to be deemed to be included within the Chaturvarna or whether it was to be a fifth varna quite distinct from the original four varnas. All this is quite clear. What is, however, not clear is the class to which it refers. This is because Manu makes no specific mention of the class involved in the controversy.

The verse is also enigmatic because of the ambiguity in the decision given by Manu. Manu's decision is that there is no fifth varna. As a general proposition it has a meaning which everybody can understand. But what does this decision mean in the concrete application to the class whose status was the subject matter of controversy. Obviously it is capable of two interpretations. It may mean that as according to the scheme of Chaturvarna there is no fifth varna the class in question must be deemed to belong to one of the four recognized varnas. But it may also mean that as in the original Varna System there is no provision for a fifth varna the class in question must be deemed to be outside the Varna System altogether.

The traditional interpretation adopted by the orthodox Hindu is that the statement in Manu refers to the Untouchables, that it was the Untouchables whose status was in controversy and that it was their status which is the subject-matter of Manu's decision. This interpretation is so firmly established that it has given rise to a division of Hindus into two classes called by different names, Savarnas or Hindus (those included in the Chaturvarna) and Avarnas or Untouchables (those excluded from the Chaturvarna). The question is, is this view correct? To whom does the text refer? Does it refer to the Untouchables? A discussion of this question may appear to be out of place and remote from the question under consideration. But it is not so. For if the text does refer to the Untouchables then it follows that Untouchability did exist in the time of Manu—a conclusion which touches the very heart of the question under consideration. The matter must, therefore, be thrashed out.

I am sure this interpretation is wrong. I hold that the passage does not refer to the Untouchables at all. Manu does not say which was the fifth class whose status was in controversy and about whose status he has given a decision in this passage. Was it the class of Untouchables or was it some other class? In support of my conclusion that the passage does not refer to Untouchables at all I rely on two circumstances. In the first place, there was no Untouchability in the time of Manu. There was only Impurity. Even the Chandala for whom Manu has nothing but contempt is only an impure person. That being so, this passage cannot possibly have any 'reference to Untouchables'. In the second place, there is evidence to support the view that this passage has reference to slaves and not to Untouchables. This view is based on the language of the passage quoted from the *Narada Smriti* in the chapter on the Occupational Theory of Untouchability.[9] It will be noticed that the *Narada Smriti* speaks of the slaves as the fifth class. If the expression fifth class in the *Narada Smriti* refers to slaves, I see no reason why the expression fifth class in *Manusmriti* should not be taken to have reference to slaves. If this reasoning is correct, it cuts at the very root of the contention that Untouchability existed in the time of Manu and that Manu was not prepared to include them as part of the Varna System. For the reasons stated, the passage does not refer to Untouchability and there is, therefore, no reason to conclude that there was Untouchability in the time of Manu.

Thus we can be sure of fixing the upper limit for the date of the birth of Untouchability. We can definitely say that *Manusmriti* did not enjoin Untouchability. There, however, remains one important question. What is the date of *Manusmriti*? Without an answer to this question it would not be possible for the average person to relate the existence or non-existence of Untouchability to any particular point in time. There is no unanimity among savants regarding the date of *Manusmriti*. Some regard it as very ancient and some regard it as very recent. After taking all facts into consideration Prof Bühler has fixed a date which appears to strike the truth. According to Bühler, *Manusmriti* in the shape in which it exists now, came into existence in the Second Century AD.[10] In assigning so recent a date to the *Manusmriti* Prof Bühler is not quite alone. Mr Daphtary[11] has also come to the same conclusion. According to him *Manusmriti* came into being after the year 185 BC and not before. The reason given by Mr Daphtary is that *Manusmriti* has a close connection with the murder of the Buddhist Emperor Brihadratha of the Maurya dynasty by his Brahmin Commander-in-Chief Pushyamitra Sunga and as even that took place in 185 BC, he concludes that *Manusmriti* must have been written after 185 BC. To give support to so important a conclusion it is necessary to establish a nexus between the murder of Brihadratha Maurya by Pushyamitra and the writing of *Manusmriti* by strong and convincing evidence. Mr Daphatry has unfortunately omitted to do so. Consequently his conclusion appears to hang in the air. The establishment of such a nexus is absolutely essential. Fortunately there is no want of evidence for the purpose.

The murder of Brihadratha Maurya by Pushyamitra[12] has unfortunately passed unnoticed. At any rate it has not received the attention it deserves. It is treated by historians as an ordinary incident between two individuals as though its origin lay in some personal quarrel between the two. Having regard to its consequences it was an epoch-making event. Its significance cannot be measured by treating it as a change of dynasty—the Sungas succeeding the Mauryas. It was a political revolution as great as the French Revolution, if not greater. It was a revolution—a bloody revolution—engineered by the Brahmins to overthrow the rule of the Buddhist Kings. That is what the murder of Brihadratha by

Pushyamitra means.

This triumphant Brahmanism was in need of many things. It of course needed to make Chaturvarna the law of the land the validity of which was denied by the Buddhists. It needed to make animal sacrifice, which was abolished by the Buddhists, legal. But it needed more than this. Brahmanism in bringing about this revolution against the rule of the Buddhist Kings had transgressed two rules of the customary law of the land which were accepted by all as sacrosanct and inviolable. The first rule made it a sin for a Brahmin even to touch a weapon. The second made the King's person sacred and regicide a sin. Triumphant Brahmanism wanted a sacred text, infallible in its authority, to justify their transgressions. A striking feature of the *Manusmriti* is that it not only makes Chaturvarna the law of the land, it not only makes animal sacrifice legal but it goes to state when a Brahmin could justifiably resort to arms and when he could justifiably kill the King. In this the *Manusmriti* has done what no prior Smriti has done. It is a complete departure. It is a new thesis. Why should the *Manusmriti* do this? The only answer is, it had to strengthen the revolutionary deeds committed by Pushyamitra by propounding philosophic justification. This interconnection between Pushyamitra and the new thesis propounded by Manu shows that the *Manusmriti* came into being sometime after 185 BC, a date not far removed from the date assigned by Prof Bühler. Having got the date of the *Manusmriti* we can say that in the Second Century AD, there was no Untouchability.

Now to turn to the possibility of determining the lower limit to the birth of Untouchability. For this we must go to the Chinese travellers who are known to have visited India and placed on record what they saw of the modes and manners of the Indian people. Of these Chinese travellers Fa-Hian[13] has something very interesting to say. He came to India in 400 AD. In the course of his observations occurs the following passage:[14]

> Southward from this [Mathura] is the so-called middle-country (Madhyadesa). The climate of this country is warm and equable, without frost or snow. The people are very well off, without poll-tax or official restrictions. Only those who till the royal lands return a portion of profit of the land. If they desire to go, they go; if they like to stop they stop. The kings govern without corporal punishment; criminals are fined, according to circumstances, lightly or heavily. Even in cases of repeated rebellion they only cut off the right hand. The King's personal attendants, who guard him on the right and left, have fixed salaries. Throughout the country the people kill no living thing nor drink wine, nor do they eat garlic or onion, with the exception of Chandalas only. The Chandalas are named 'evil men' and dwell apart from others; if they enter a town or market, they sound a piece of wood in order to separate themselves; then, men knowing they are [near], avoid coming in contact with them. In this country they do not keep swine nor fowls, and do not deal in cattle; they have no shambles or wine shops in their market-places. In selling they use cowrie shells. The Chandalas only hunt and sell flesh.

Can this passage be taken as evidence of the prevalence of Untouchability at the time of Fa-Hian? Certain parts of his description of the treatment given to the Chandalas do seem to lend support to the conclusion, that is, a case of Untouchability. There is, however, one difficulty in the way of accepting this conclusion. The difficulty arises because the facts relate to the Chandalas. The Chandala is not a good case to determine the existence or non-existence of Untouchability. The Brahmins have regarded the Chandalas as their hereditary enemies and are prone to attribute to them abominable conduct; hurl at them low epithets and manufacture towards them a mode of behaviour which is utterly artificial to suit their venom against them. Whatever, therefore, is said against the Chandalas must be taken with considerable reservations.

This argument is not based on mere speculation. Those who doubt its cogency may consider the evidence of Bana's[15] *Kadambari*[16] for a different description of the treatment accorded to the Chandalas.

The story of Kadambari is a very complex one and we are really not concerned with it. It is enough for our purpose to note that the story is told to king Shudraka by a parrot named Vaishampayana who was the pet of a Chandala girl. The following passages from the Kadambari are important for our purpose. It is better to begin with Bana's description of a Chandala settlement. It is in the following terms:[17]

> I beheld the barbarian settlement, a very market-place of evil deeds. It was surrounded on all sides by boys engaged in the chase, unleashing their hounds, teaching their falcons, mending snares, carrying weapons, and fishing, horrible in their attire, like demoniacs. Here and there the entrance to their dwellings, hidden by thick bamboo forests, was to be inferred, from the rising of smoke of orpiment. On all sides the enclosures were made with skulls; (627) the dust-heaps on the roads were filled with bones; the yards of the huts were miry with blood, fat, and meat chopped up. The life there consisted of hunting; the food, of flesh; the ointment, of fat; the garments, of coarse silk; the couches, of dried skins; the household attendants, of dogs; the animals for riding, of cows; the men's employment, of wine and women; the oblation to the gods, of blood; the sacrifice, of cattle. The

place was the image of all hells.

It is from such a settlement that the Chandala girl starts with her parrot to the palace of king Shudraka. King Shudraka is sitting in the Hall of Audience with his Chieftains. ... The king and the Chieftains did not at first take notice of her. To attract attention she struck a bamboo on the mosaic floor to arouse the King. Bana then proceeds to describe her appearance.

> Then the king, with the words, 'Look yonder' to his suite, gazed steadily upon the Candala maiden, as she was pointed out by the portress; Before her went a man, whose hair was hoary with age, whose eyes were the colour of the red lotus, whose joints, despite the loss of youth, were firm from incessant labour, whose form, though that of Matanga,[18] was not to be despised, and who wore the white raiment meet for a court. Behind her went a Candala boy, with locks falling on either shoulder, bearing a cage, the bars of which, though of gold, shone like emerald from the reflection of the parrot's plumage. She herself seemed by the darkness of her hue to imitate Krishna when he guilefully assumed a woman's attire to take away the amrita seized by the demons. She was, as it were, a doll of sapphire walking alone; and over the blue garment, which reached to her ankle, there fell a veil of red silk, like evening sunshine falling on blue lotuses. The circle of her cheek was whitened by the ear-ring that hung from one ear, like the face of night inlaid with the rays of the rising moon; she had a tawny tilaka of gorocana, as if it were a third eye, like Parvati in mountaineer's attire, after the fashion of the garb of Siva.
>
> She was like Sri darkened by the sapphire glory of Narayana reflected on the robe on her breast; or like Rati, stained by smoke which rose as Madana was burnt by the fire of wrathful Civa; or like Yamuna, fleeing in fear of being drawn along by

the ploughshare of wild Balarama; or, from the rich lac that turned her lotus feet into budding shoots, like Durga, with her feet crimsoned by the blood of the Asura Mahisha she had just trampled upon.

Her nails were rosy from the pink glow of her fingers; the mosaic pavement seemed too hard for her touch, and she came forward, placing her feet like tender twigs upon the ground ...[19]

... And the king was amazed; and the thought arose in his mind, 'Ill-placed was the labour of the Creator in producing this beauty! For if she has been created as though in mockery of her Candala form, such that all the world's wealth of loveliness is laughed to scorn by her own, why was she born in a race with which none can mate? Surely by thought alone did Prajapati create her, fearing the penalties of contact with the Matanga race, else whence this unsullied radiance, a grace that belongs not to limbs sullied by touch? Moreover, though fair in form, by the baseness of her birth, whereby she, like a Lakshmi of the lower world, is a perpetual reproach to the gods, she, lovely as she is, causes fear in Brahma, the maker of so strange a union.' ...

On reading this description of a Chandala girl many questions arise. Firstly, how different it is from the description given by Fa-Hian?[20] Secondly Bana is a Vatsyayana Brahmin.[21]

This Vatsyayana Brahmin, after giving a description of the Chandala settlement, finds no compunction in using such eloquent and gorgeous language to describe the Chandala girl. Is this description compatible with the sentiments of utter scorn and contempt associated with Untouchability? If the Chandalas were Untouchables how could an Untouchable girl enter the King's palace? How could an Untouchable be described in the superb terms used by Bana? Far from being degraded, the Chandalas of Bana's period had Ruling Families among them. For Bana speaks of the Chandala girl as a Chandala princess[22] Bana wrote some time about 600 AD, and by 600 AD the Chandalas had not come to be regarded as Untouchables. It is, therefore, quite possible that the conditions described by Fa-Hian, though bordering on Untouchability, may not be taken as amounting to Untouchability. It may only be the extreme form of impurity practised by the Brahmins who are always in the habit of indulging in overdoing their part in sacerdotalism. This becomes more than plausible if we remember that when Fa-Hian came to India it was the reign of the Gupta Kings. The Gupta Kings were patrons of Brahmanism. It was a period of the triumph and revival of Brahmanism. It is quite possible that what Fa-Hian describes is not Untouchability but an extremity to which the Brahmins were prepared to carry the ceremonial impurity which had become attached to some community, particularly to the Chandalas.

The next Chinese traveller who came into India was Yuan Chwang. He came to India in 629 AD. He stayed in India for 16 years and has left most accurate records of journeys up and down the country and of the manners and customs of the people. In the course of his description of general characters of the cities and buildings of India, he says:[23]

> As to their inhabited towns and cities the quadrangular walls of the cities (or according to one text, of the various regions) are broad and high, while the thoroughfares arc narrow tortuous passages. The shops are on the highways and booths (or, inns) line the roads. Butchers, fishermen, public performers, executioners, and scavengers have their habitations marked by a distinguishing sign. They are forced to live outside the city and they sneak along on the left when

going about in the hamlets.

The above passage is too short and too brief for founding a definite conclusion thereon. There is, however, one point about it which is worthy of note. Fa-Hian's description refers to the Chandalas only while the description given by Yuan Chwang applies to communities other than the Chandalas. This is a point of great importance. No such argument can be levelled against the acceptance of a description since it applies to communities other than the Chandalas. It is, therefore, just possible that when Yuan Chwang came to India, Untouchability had emerged.

On the basis of what has been said above we can conclude that while Untouchability did not exist in 200 AD, it had emerged by 600 AD.

These are the two limits, upper and lower, for determining the birth of Untouchability. Can we fix an approximate date for the birth of Untouchability? I think we can, if we take beef-eating, which is the root of Untouchability, as the point to start from. Taking the ban on beef-eating as a point to reconnoitre from, it follows that the date of the birth of Untouchability must be intimately connected with the ban on cow-killing and on eating beef. If we can answer when cow-killing became an offence and beef-eating became a sin, we can fix an approximate date for the birth of Untouchability.

When did cow-killing become an offence?

We know that Manu did not prohibit the eating of beef nor did he make cow-killing an offence. When did it become an offence? As has been shown by Dr D.R. Bhandarkar, cow killing was made a capital offence by the Gupta kings sometime in the 4th Century AD.

We can, therefore, say with some confidence that Untouchability was born some time about 400 AD. It is born out of the struggle for supremacy between Buddhism and Brahmanism which has so completely moulded the history of India and the study of which is so woefully neglected by students of Indian history.

Notes

Preface

1 Ambedkar's *Who were the Shudras?*, first published in 1946, two years before the publication of *The Untouchables: Who Were They and Why They Became Untouchables?*, charts a history of the emergence of the Shudra varna. He hypothesizes that no such varna existed to begin with. It was a feud between Kshatriyas and Brahmins that eventually led the warrior caste to lose their status and become Shudras.

2 The classification of entire communities as 'Criminal Tribes' was in large part an effect of colonialism. After the Revolt of 1857, an extensive census was conducted by the British to take stock of newly acquired territories. Bands of roaming dacoits abounded, and these were turned into an ethnic category, following the logic of caste, which they were led to believe dictated every social and occupational activity. Over two hundred communities were labelled 'Criminal Tribes' through the Criminal Tribes Act, 1871. They were treated as habitual criminals, and were harshly monitored and disciplined. After independence, the so-called criminal tribes were 'de-notified' and are now known as Denotified Tribes (DNTs); but the stigma of 'thugee' in Indian popular imagination remains. In the fight against continued repression, the moniker 'Vimukta jatis' has been adopted by several members of the community (Bajrange et al. 2018; Schwarz 2010).

3 The word 'aborigine' was used by European colonizers as a catch-all term to unify the multiplicity of cultures across the world into a position of lowliness. In India, 'Aboriginal Tribes', now termed as 'Scheduled Tribes', was again used to denote a multiplicity of cultures: from the tribes in Nagaland to those in Kerala. This denotation only arises when one sees Hinduism as the superior order against which all the various tribal practices

are juxtaposed as inferior. It is the rise of caste and Brahmanism with its need to expand and assimilate differences into a singular order that gave rise to a subjectivity such as 'Adivasi' and 'aboriginal', relegating them to outside the fold. Ambedkar's understanding of tribal communities was influenced largely by prejudicial colonial interpretations in his time (Duncan 2005).

4 Voltaire was the pen-name of François-Marie d'Arouet (1694–1778), a leading figure of European Enlightenment in the eighteenth century. Though primarily a writer and activist, his philosophical tracts had a profound impact on Western thought. His thought was concerned with individual human liberty, hedonistic ethics of voluptuousness, scepticism and a belief in Newtonian empirical science (Shank 2015). Voltaire's antisemitism, racism and participation in the slave trade have led to a re-evaluation of his legacy in recent times (Harvey 2012; Poliakov 2003: 88–89).

5 Johann Wolfgang von Goethe (1749–1832) was a poet, dramatist and novelist who came to symbolize the Germany of his times more than any other figure. Philosopher Robert Solomon writes about Goethe, '[His] rich and varied life, as a conservative and libertine, as a young lawyer and as author-autocrat of Weimar, as an artist, a scientist, and above all, a poet, has often been compared to the rich and varied experience of Germany from the first waves of chauvinism and sentiment with the poet Klopstock to the beginnings of militaristic nationalism' (Solomon 1983: 37n2).

6 [*Maxims and Reflections of Goethe*, Nos. 453, 543.] *Maxims and Reflections of Goethe* is a collection of aphorisms that Goethe put together in the later period of his life on varied subjects like life and character, literature and art, science and nature.

7 Mountstuart Elphinstone (1779–1859) was a Scottish diplomat and statesman who served the East India Company as envoy to Kabul and in the court of the Peshwas, before the Anglo–Maratha Wars. He was later appointed as Lieutenant-Governor of the Bombay province (Cotton 1911).

8 The quote is from Elphinstone's magnum opus *The History of India* (1843: 19), which was written to build on the colonial understanding of

the subcontinent which stemmed from James Mill's *The History of British India* (1817).

9 Maxim Gorky (1868–1936) was a leading figure of social-realist literature in pre-revolutionary Russia. He was praised for the simplicity of his writing and for his depiction of the indignity of working-class life. His style became prototypical of the kind of literature expected from revolutionary writers (Tikhonov 1946).

10 [*Literature and Life. A selection from the writings of Maxim Gorky.*] The quote is taken from an essay entitled "How I Learnt to Write" (Gorky 1982: 31).

Chapter IX

1 In the 1901 Census report under the commissionership of ethno-grapher H.H. Risley, considerable attention was paid to distinguish animism from Hinduism. Risley regarded animism as a lower order religion reducible to belief in magic, whereas Hinduism for him was distinguishable through its transcendental metaphysics (Risley and Gait 1901: 357–59). Risley found it difficult to precisely pin down the definition of Hinduism, mired as it is in a multiplicity of beliefs and practices. His eventual definition of it was not too wide off the mark: 'The most obvious characteristics of the ordinary Hindu are his acceptance of the Brahmanical supremacy and of the caste system, and when it is a question of whether a member of the Animistic tribes has or has not entered the fold of Hinduism, this seems the proper test to apply' (1901: 360). The Census Commissioner for 1911, when the animists and Untouchables were seen as separate from the Hindus, was E.A. Gait, co-author of the 1901 report with Risley.

2 The 1931 Census was the last to enumerate all castes; following the Census Act of 1948, only the Scheduled Castes and Tribes were enumerated by caste. Ahead of the 2001 Census, it was under consideration if caste was a category appropriate for the census. The debate was renewed in 2011 (Deshpande and John 2010) and the Socio Economic and Caste Census (SECC) was conducted as part of the 2011 Census.

3 The Shimla Deputation, a meeting where thirty-five Muslim leaders met with the Viceroy Lord Minto to press for separate representation, actually happened in October 1906.

4 Sir Sultan Muhammed Shah, Aga Khan III (1877–1957), was one of the founders and the first president of the All-India Muslim League. His petition to the then viceroy resulted in the Minto–Morley reforms, or the Indian Councils Act of 1909.

5 [For the text of the address see my *Pakistan*, p. 431]. In *Pakistan or the Partition of India* (1945), Ambedkar writes: 'These demands were granted and given effect to in the Act of 1909. Under this Act the Mohammedans were given (1) the right to elect their representatives, (2) the right to elect their representatives by separate electorates, (3) the right to vote in the general electorates as well, and (4) the right to weightage in representation' (Ambedkar 1990c: 251).

6 [Italics not in the original.]

7 It is a commonly held view that the creation of Pakistan was largely down to the machinations of Muhammad Ali Jinaah. See Jaffrelot 2002 for a critique of this argument. See Jalal 1985 for a history of majority–minority demographic concerns that enabled a popular movement for Pakistan. Faisal Devji (2013) presents an alternate view of how religion functioned as ideology to create a new imagined national community. Ambedkar's *Pakistan or the Partition of India* (1945) was a key text that presented detailed arguments both for and against the creation of Pakistan. The book was a bestseller, and was used by both Jinnah and the Congress to press their points.

8 [This operation came soon after the address given by the Muslim community to Lord Minto in 1909 in which they asked for a separate and adequate representation for the Muslim community. The Hindu smelt a rat in it. As the Census Commissioner observed: 'Incidentally, the enquiry generated a certain amount of heat, because unfortunately it happened to be made at a time when the rival claims of Hindus and Mohammedans to

representation on the Legislative Councils were being debated and some of the former feared that it would lead to the exclusion of certain classes from the category of Hindus and would thus react unfavourably on their political importance'. Part I. p. 116.]

9 [See Census of India (1911). Part 1. p. 117]

10 In the present time, an opposite process is underway: to assimilate Adivasis into the Hindu fold. The Rashtriya Swayamsevak Sangh and allied organizations refer to them as 'vanvasi' (literally, forest-dwellers), and are replacing their traditional practices with Sangh-approved Hindu rituals. This is also an attempt to counter the influence of Christian missionaries on tribal communities. To this effect, the Vanvasi Kalyan Ashram has been set up, to promote their own version of ideological education. See Sundar 2002.

11 Surprisingly, Ambedkar leaves out the criterion of burying the dead, a tradition that followed by his own Mahar jati. He does mention this fact in his essay "The Mahars: Who Were They and How They Became Untouchable?" (Ambedkar 2003).

12 [See Census of 1911 for Assam p. 40; for Bengal, Bihar and Orisa p. 282; for CP. p. 73; for Madras p. 51; for Punjab p. 109; for U.P. p. 121; for Baroda p. 55; for Mysore p. 53; for Rajputana p. 94—105; for Travancore p. 198]

13 [*Hindu Manners and Customs* (3rd Edition) p. 61 f.n.] Jean-Antoine Dubois or Abbé Dubois (1765–1848) was a French missionary who arrived in Pondicherry in the wake of the French Revolution on a proselytizing mission. His book *Character, Manners and Customs of the People of India and of their Institutions Religious and Civil*, which was written after his travels across South India and influenced by his Brahmin interlocuters, became an influential ethnographic text for both British and French colonial governance.

14 The Paraiyars and Pallars are the most numerous Dalit castes in the Tamil-speaking region of the erstwhile Madras presidency. Rupa Viswanath

(2014) notes that the Paraiyars were agrestic slaves until the colonial period, forced into a range of menial occupations in the northern districts of the state. The Pallars, predominant in the southern regions, were farm workers, though today some of their spokespersons claim they were originally wetland farmers and even rulers (Krishnasamy 2018). The Chakkiliyars, who have now embraced the more 'respectable' though Hinduized label of 'Arundhatiyar', are traditionally leather workers predominant in the western districts of the state.

15 [Gazetteer of Tanjore District (1906), p. 80] M.C. Rajah writes in *The Oppressed Hindus* (1925), which is considered the first-ever English-language nonfiction book written by a Dalit: 'It is not so well known that the Brahmin who considers himself polluted by the touch, the presence or the shadow of an Adi Dravida, will not be allowed to enter the *Cheri-natham*. Should a Brahmin venture into a *cheri*, water with which cow dung has been mixed, is thrown on his head and he is driven out. Some Brahmins consider a forsaken *cheri*, an auspicious site for an *agraharam*' (Rajah 1925/2005).

16 Holeyas, belonging to the present-day state of Karnataka and its adjoining regions, are primarily agricultural labourers.

17 Little is known of James Stuart Francis Fraser Mackenzie except that he was a colonial official who worked in Mysore and Southern India. He authored several scholarly essays (including the much-cited "The Village Feast," in the *Indian Antiquary* in 1874 which describes a fire-walking ritual in Akka Timanhully in Bangalore as largely benign and harmless) and nine books from the 1870s to the 1910s.

18 [*Indian Antiquary* 1873 11.65.] Some errors in spelling and punctuation in the BAWS edition have been edited after comparing with Mackenzie's essay in the *Indian Antiquary*. The quote also appears in the second volume of Edgar Thurston and K. Rangachari's *Castes and Tribes of Southern India* (1909).

19 The Broken Men theory is Ambedkar's novel explanation of the origin of Untouchability in India. It can be summarized in three points:

1. Primitive tribal society could be divided into two categories: Settled (which practised agriculture) and Nomadic.
2. The Nomadic communities found it favourable to attack Settled Tribes for resources and food. This created a community of 'Broken Men': people who lost their homes and were left tribe-less.
3. Since Broken Men couldn't assimilate into other communities in a kinship based society, they could only establish themselves outside other settled village, who would provide them with food in lieu of defensive services. These communities ended up becoming modern-day Untouchables.

20 In *Haunting the Buddha: Indian Popular Religions and the Formation of Buddhism* (2004), Robert DeCaroli argues that Buddhism became a mass religion, not by opposing extant religious practices as is popularly assumed, but by subsuming the worship of spirit-deities and the dead into its own liturgy.

21 Nilakantha Bhatta was a seventeenth-century philosopher best known for his encyclopaedic interpretation of Brahmanic laws collected together in the Mayukhas ('rays of light'), which drew from various canonical sources, including the *Manusmriti*, to provide a consistent rulebook for the dwijas.

22 [Edited by Gharpure, p. 95] Ambedkar is citing from his *Santi Mayukha: A Treatise on Propitiatory Rituals* by Bhatta Nilakantha, self-published by J.R. Gharpure in Sanskrit in 1924. Of Nilakantha's twelve Mayukhas, *Prayaschit Mayukha* is the tenth. It details the various ways in which sin and pollution can occur in caste society, the punishments that await sinners in hell and the means of repentance. The Mayukhas were popular books of Hindu ethics in Gujarat, Konkan and Maharashtra, and are said to have been brought into prominence by the Marathas in the seventeenth and eighteenth centuries (Macnaghten 1860; Mitra 1881).

23 Apararka, or Aparaditya, was a monarch of the Shilahara dynasty who ruled over the Konkan region in the late twelfth century. He is best known for *Apararka-Yajnavalkya-Dharma-sastra nibandha*, his commentary on the *Yajnavalkya Smriti*, which is the second most important Smriti after the *Manusmriti*.

24 [*Smriti Sammuchaya* I. p. 118]

25 Harita was an ancient composer of Dharma Sutras who is said to have lived anywhere between 600 and 300 BCE. The two main texts attributed to him are *Vrddha Harita* and *Laghu Harita*. The *Vrddha Harita*, which comprises eight chapters and about 2,600 verses, details the obligatory duties of each varna. It is also a theoretical study of the nature of the self and it lists the various means by which one can attain moksha.

26 The treatment of Buddhist characters in Sanskrit dramas is not uniform. Bharata in his *Natyashastra* states that Buddhist monks should be addressed as 'bhadanta' or Blessed Sir. In the bhana play (a one-act monologue) *Padmaprabhrutakam* by Sudraka, the protagonist Sharvilaka makes love to a shakyabhikshaki, a Buddhist nun. In Bhavabhuti's romantic play *Malati-Madhava*, a Buddhist nun, Kamandaki, helps unite the hero and the heroine (Varadpande 2005).

27 Ambedkar appears to misread the play to make it work for his thesis. *Mricchakatika* (The Little Clay Cart), composed in the second century BCE by Sudraka, is classified as a prakarna (realistic) play reflecting society and its ordinary characters. In it, the protagonist Charudatta, a Brahmin merchant fallen upon hard times, loves a wealthy, beautiful courtesan, Vasantsena, who in turn is pursued by the king's ill-bred brother-in-law, Sakara, also the local governor. In the scene that Ambedkar discusses, the role of social distinctions are reflected in the depiction of the Buddhist monk to satirize this reality. The attitude towards Buddhists is not universally hostile in the play. The scene that riles Ambedkar serves to further the comic element and Sakara's villainous character rather than establish the inferiority of Buddhists. Though *Mricchakatika* may not be itself contemptuous towards Buddhism, that the element of contempt does exist, in the mind of a character, is of use for Ambedkar's purpose. See Kosambi 2008, for a reading of the play as dissident rather than orthodox.

28 In the 1905 translation of the play by Arthur William Ryder, and in all other translations, we see that the courtier Vita brazenly mocking Sakara, is referred to as Sansthanaka (the governor). Vita addresses the loutish

governor not as 'Friend' but as 'You jackass' (as he does in almost every other scene he shares with him) three times in the course of the scene. Vita admonishes Sakara for going after a harmless monk. In fact, in almost all the scenes involving the courtier and the governor, the latter is shown to be a comic villain who exercises brute authority.

29 At the end of *Mrichhakatika*, the Brahmin Charudatta is indeed sentenced to death, contrary to Ambedkar's claim. However, in keeping with his reading, Charudatta is pardoned in the final act thanks to the Buddhist monk Samvahaka's intervention.

30 Popular theories of Buddhist decline point to the growing decadence of the monastery after its adoption by the gentry, the appropriation of Buddhist tenets of ahimsa into the Brahmanic religion, and the emergence of figures like Adi Shankara. In another text, "The Decline and Fall of Buddhism" (1987a: 229–38), Ambedkar also endorses the view that Muslim invaders played a role in the disappearance of Buddhism. Gail Omvedt (2003) rejects all these theories as 'facile generalisations' given the lack of substantial evidence, but agrees that persecution may indeed have played a role in the decline of the religion, based on Hsuan Tsang's account of violence against Buddhists. More recently, historian Douglas Ober (2023) has shown that accounts of the disappearance of Buddhism are greatly exaggerated; though there was a decline in its status, he argues that there is credible evidence for us to assume that Buddhism was very much alive and thriving in different regions of medieval South Asia through the thirteenth to eighteenth centuries.

Chapter X

1 Shalini Randeria (1989) shows that access to the dead cow was secured through a system of taxation. In medieval Gujarat, Untouchables had to pay a tax known as *bhambh* (literally, dead animal) to have the right of access to carrion and flay its skin. A similar system existed in Maharashtra where Mahars were allotted a *watan* to carry out similar tasks (Kotani 1997a; Kotani 1997b).

2 [The Untouchables have felt the force of the accusation levelled against them by the Hindus for eating beef. Instead of giving up the habit, the Untouchables have invented a philosophy which justifies eating the beef of the dead cow. The gist of the philosophy is that eating the flesh of the dead cow is a better way of showing respect to the cow than throwing her carcass to the wind.]

3 Vyasa was a mythic sage who is credited with the authorship of the Mahabharata and for rendering the Vedas in their present four-part structure. In addition, he is said to have composed the Puranas and the Upapuranas. He was also the originator of the Brahmin tradition of 'smriti': the practice of writing down that which is passed down orally (Sullivan 1990). We have not been able establish the provenance of the *Veda Vyas Smriti*.

4 [Quoted in Kane's *History of Dharmasastras*, Vol. II, Part 1, p. 71.] The following quote appears in its original Sanskrit form in Kane's text (1941). Kane here discusses the term Antyaja and all its various occurrences and cadences across the Shastras. It is possible that Ambedkar has translated the extract himself based on the explanation Kane provides in pages 70–71 of the *History of Dharmasastras*.

Chapter XI

1 The Rig Veda, considered the most important of the four Vedas, is one of the oldest surviving texts in human history, dated to 1200–1500 BCE. It is divided into ten mandalas (chapters) and contains 1,017 suktas with eleven additional 'khilas'. Most of the hymns take the form of praises and were chanted during sacrifices, which involved slaughter of animals and their burning on a sacrificial fire, to invoke deities like Indra, Agni, Soma and Varuna. The Purusha Sukta hymn, found in the tenth book, contains the first known articulation of the four major social groups (varna) along with their symbolic functions (Mani 1975). In most of his works, Ambedkar refers to *Rig-Veda Sanhita* compiled and translated by Horace Hayman Wilson from 1850–88 (6 vols), though he does not always provide citations. All further references here are from the Jamison and Brereton edition of 2014.

2 'Making the sound *hin*, the goods-mistress of goods, seeking her calf, has come near through (my) thinking/ Let this inviolable cow give milk to the Asvins. Let her increase for our great good fortune' (Jamison and Brereton 2014: 357).

3 'Of this well-portioned god here his manifestation is the fairest, the most brilliant one among mortals/ Gleaming like the heated ghee of the inviolable (cow), (the manifestation) of the god is eagerly sought like the largesse of a milk-cow' (Jamison and Brereton 2014: 557).

4 V.82.8 makes no reference to the cow, and sukta 82 is about the 'Savitar'. V.84.8 offers the closest match: 'The great bucket—turn it up, pour it down. Let the brooks, unleashed, flow forward/ Inundate Heaven and Earth with ghee. Let there be a good watering hole for the prized cows' (Jamison and Brereton 2014: 766).

5 There's no verse at VII.69.71, but there's VII.69, focused on Asvins, featuring eight verses with none referring to a cow. A proximate verse is VII.68.9: 'This praise-poet here awakens with good hymns, rousing himself at the beginning of the dawns, bringing good thoughts./ The fertile cow makes him grow strong with her refreshing drink, with her milk. – Do you protect us always with your blessings' (Jamison and Brereton 2014: 968).

6 'A year's worth of the milk of the ruddy cow: let the sorcerer not eat of that, o you with your eye on men. Whoever seeks to gorge himself on [/ steal] the beestings, with your flame pierce him face-to-face in his vulnerable spot, o Agni' (Jamison and Brereton 2014: 1531).

7 The hymn begins with: 'The cows have come here and have made (the house) blessed. Let them find a place in the cow-stall; let them find enjoyment among us'; but verse three makes it clear that only the sacrificer (the Hotar Brahmin) has absolute rights over his cows: 'Those (cows) with which he sacrifices and gives to the gods, he keeps company with them as their cowherd for a very long time' (Jamison and Brereton 2014: 812).

8 'Mother of the Rudras, daughter of the Vasus, sister of the Adityas, navel of immortality—/ I now proclaim to observant people: do not smite the

blameless cow—Aditi' (Jamison and Brereton 2014: 1213).

9 Brahmanas are instruction manuals for performing Vedic rituals that form the second literary stratum of the Vedas, after the Samhitas. The *Aitareya Brahmana* and *Satapatha Brahmana* (Brahmanas of one hundred parts) are the most important ones, the latter being the most recent. They indicate a shift from an emphasis on the importance of ritual to invoke gods to stressing the power of rituals in and of themselves (Lochtefeld 2002: 122).

10 'At first, namely, the gods offered up a man as the victim. When he was offered up, the sacrificial essence went out of him. It entered into the horse. They offered up the horse. When it was offered up, the sacrificial essence went out of it. It entered into the ox. They offered up the ox. When it was offered up, the sacrificial essence went out of it. It entered into the sheep. They offered up the sheep. When it was offered up, the sacrificial essence went out of it. It entered into the goat. They offered up the goat. When it was offered up, the sacrificial essence went out of it' (Eggeling 1882: 50).

11 Apastamba was a sage, writer and commentator. The Dharma Sutra that bears his name (roughly 400 BCE) is a major source for the law code attributed to Manu which was considered a traditional source of Hindu law by the British rulers. Dharma Sutras, the earliest literature of dharma, are in prose, unlike the versified Dharmasastras which succeeded them.

12 The reference to the verse is erroneous. Ambedkar may be referring to I.17.29 in the *Apastamba Dharma Sutra*: 'The meat of one-hoofed animals, camels, Gayal oxen, village pigs, and Sarabha cattle are forbidden' (Olivelle 1999: 28). The very next verse reads: 'It is permitted to eat the meat of milch cows and oxen./ A text of the Vajasaneyins states: "The meat of oxen is fit for sacrifice"' (I.17.30–31).

13 Ludwig Alsdorf (2010) points out the Iranian origin of the word 'Aghnya'; the Persian word for cow was 'agznya'. He suggests that the word indicates 'that which cannot be killed', rather than 'that which must not be killed'. Sebastian Carri (2000) indicates two other interpretations of 'Aghnya' made by Hanns-Peter Schmidt, a German Indo-Iranist and

scholar of Sanskrit: as the tame animal par excellence (domestic rather than wild) and as that which is characterized by its non-killing, i.e. life-giving, nurturing nature.

14 Pandurang Vaman Kane (1880–1972) was an Indologist and Sanskritist. He was given the honorific of Mahamahopadhyaya in 1941, won the Sahitya Akademi award for his *History of Dharmasastras, Volume IV*, in 1956 and was bestowed with the Bharat Ratna in 1963. Nominated by the then President Rajendra Prasad, Kane served as a member of parliament in the Rajya Sabha from 1953 to 1959.

15 In the Vedas, the Samhitas form the central and most ancient layer of text. The mantras collected within the various Samhitas include hymns, benedictions, prayers, spells and litanies usually directed towards a Vedic deity (Lochtefeld 2002).

16 [*Dharm Shastra Vichar* (Marathi) p. 180]

17 '[Indra:] "For they cook fifteen, twenty oxen at a time for me. And I eat only the fat meat. They fill both my cheeks." – Above all Indra!' (Jamison and Brereton 2014: 1528).

18 '(For him) into whom horses, bulls, oxen, mated cows, rams, once released, are poured out [=offered] ...' (Jamison and Brereton 2014: 1542).

19 The reference Ambedkar makes here does not have any mention of cow slaughter. The hymn to which the verse belongs extolls the marauding prowess of the Aryas, mythically embodied in the figures of Indra and Manu. One can argue that it alludes to a sort of cow-sacrifice; however, the layers of metaphor imbued in the text dissuade any definitive claim.

20 The *Kamyashti*s or *Kamya Ishti*s are the minor sacrifices prescribed in the *Taittiriya Brahmana* (Chakravarti 1979).

21 Each Veda is broadly divided into four sections: Samhitas, Brahmanas, Aranyakas and Upanishads. The Vedas were studied by several rishis who went on to create their own schools and editions of the original text. These schools were known as shakhas (Mani 1975). One such shakha was the

Taittirya, which was a recension of the Krishna (Black) Yajur Veda; its origin is attributed to Yajnavalkya, the mythic sage Vyasa's disciple (Dalal 2014).

22 No such reference is found in Patrick Olivelle's translation of the *Apastamba Dharma Sutra* (1999).

23 The popular ceremony, employed for welcoming guests, is both a Srauta ritual (performed by someone versed in the srutis) and a Grihya (domestic) ritual. It is also part of Soma sacrifices (Valhe 2015).

24 The Grihya Sutras are manuals that prescribe domestic behaviours, ceremonies and rituals. Among other things, these texts outline daily sacred-fire rites and the life-cycles rites (Samskaras).

25 The Rig Veda (X.68.3) mentions the word atithinir, which has been interpreted as 'cows fit for guests' and refers to at least one Vedic hero, Atithigva, meaning literally 'slaying cows for guests' (Keith 1920: 118).

26 The Asv.gr. is the *Asvalayana Grihya Sutra*. The ingredients of the Madhuparka are mentioned in 24.5–6: 'He pours honey into curds,/ Or butter, if he can get no honey' (Oldenberg 1886: 82).

27 The reference is to the *Apastamba Grihya Sutra*.

28 The given reference in the *Paraskara Grihya Sutra* does not speak about the Madhuparka; however, at 10.5, we find: 'Let them announce three times (to the guest) separately (each of the following things which are brought to him): a bed (of grass to sit down on), water for washing the feet, the Argha water, water for sipping, and the Madhuparka (i.e. a mixture of ghee, curds, and honey)' (Oldenberg 1886: 214).

29 The *Kausika Sutra* is an accessory text to the Atharva Veda. It contains exegeses on medicinal and abhicara practices (incantations by a priest to defeat any enemy).

30 Ambedkar is probably referring to the *Manava Grihya Sutra* here. This Grihya Sutra belongs to the Manava school of the Krishna (Black) Yajur Veda. This text lists the rules that ought to be followed by a good Brahmacharin. The reference given by Ambedkar reads: 'namaanso madhuparkah iti

shrutih' [which, according to Bibek Debroy means: 'Without flesh, it is not madhuparka. The sacred texts have said this'].

31 [Kane's vol. II. Part I p. 545.] In the BAWS edition of *The Untouchables*, the above quote is given as part of Ambedkar's own text and the footnote is placed wrongly. These errors have been rectified.

32 The term 'goghna' is used by Panini, the Sanskrit grammarian, to connote 'guests'. Although, the word is used in a pejorative sense by Manu's time, its original meaning was 'one for whom the cow is killed' (Jha 2009: 33).

33 Asvalayana is the most well-known disciple of Saunaka, a celebrated teacher of the Atharva Veda. He is the founder of a Sakha of the Rig Veda, one of the many variations of the texts traditionally handed down orally by teachers, leading to the formation of different schools of interpretations. Most of his Rigvedic recensions however have been lost.

34 The following twenty-seven instructions occur in the *Asvalayana Grihya Sutra* and not the *Apastamba Grihya Sutra*. (See IV.3.1–27, Oldenberg 1886.) Ambedkar here is citing the Oldenberg translation of the Grihya Sutras, which appeared as a single volume edition in 1886. The errors in Ambedkar's version of the quote have been corrected here.

35 Yajnavalkya, the purported author of the *Yajnavalkya Smriti*, was a sage in the court of mythical king Janaka and a disciple of Sanatkumara. He is also said to have been a part of Yudhistira's court as also Indra's assembly. His works are said to have influenced the later adherents of Advaita Vedanta (Mani 1975: 891–92).

36 As far as prohibition of food is concerned, Yajnavalkya does not much differ from Manu, which points to the profound influence of the *Manusmriti* on most of the dharmshastra writers (Olivelle and Davis 2018: 26). References to the arghya, Madhuparka and rituals of welcoming learned Brahmins, indicate that consumption of consecrated meat was not merely enjoined but was necessary.

37 The Canon of Buddhist religious texts was set in its written form

around the first century BCE in Pali. The Pali Canon is divided into three sections (and therefore is known as Tipitaka, or The Three Baskets): *Vinaya Pitaka*, The Book of Discipline; *Sutta Pitaka*, the Discourses; and *Abhidhamma Pitaka*, the further doctrines. The Sutta Pitaka is divided into five further sections or Nikayas: *Digha Nikaya*, *Majjhima Nikaya*, *Samyutta Nikaya*, *Anguttara Nikaya*, and *Khuddaka Nikaya*. Of these, the *Digha Nikaya* is the longest collection and it contains thirty-four Suttas, one of which is the "Kutadanta Sutta" (Walshe 1987: 46–53).

38 The "Kutadanta Sutta" recounts the tale of the Buddha's encounter with an influential Brahmin named Kutadanta. Upon learning that the Buddha was set up in a park nearby, the Brahmin prepares 'seven hundred bulls, seven hundred bullocks, seven hundred heifers, seven hundred he-goats and seven hundred rams' in his honour, and asks the teacher what the best way to perform a sacrifice would be (Walshe 1987: 133). The Buddha then recounts the story of a king who seeks similar advice to secure good fortune. His chaplain tells him to distribute more crops and cattle to the farmers, to distribute more capital to the traders, and to increase the wages of those engaged in other services. The chaplain then tells him to summon all the Kshatriyas, advisers, counsellors, influential Brahmins and wealthy householders, and ask them to present their own sacrifices. The subjects bring the king all the wealth they have amassed as tribute. But the king refuses them saying he has no need for further wealth and asks them to keep it for themselves. The subjects, affected by the king's generosity, in turn decide to distribute what they had amassed among the people. In this vein, Kutadanta is told that the best sacrifice he can make is to accept the dhamma. Kutadanta accedes and becomes a disciple of the Buddha (Walshe 1987: 131–41).

39 The quote is taken from *Dialogues of the Buddha*, which is a translation of the *Digha Nikaya* by T.W. Rhys Davids (1899: 180).

40 Also from *Dialogues of the Buddha* (Rhys Davids 1899: 184).

41 The *Samyutta* is the third Nikaya in the *Sutta Pitaka*. It is a collection of various suttas grouped into specific categories: For instance, the reference

Ambedkar makes here is from the *Kosalasamyutta* which is a collection of dialogues the Buddha has with the Kosalan king Pasenadi. Pasenadi was the sovereign to whom the Sakhyas, the clan of the Buddha, swore fealty. Like the Magadhan kings of his time, he was of 'low-birth' and did not have tribal affiliations, leading to his ability to create a large army not based on tribal origin. He also didn't have much regard for Vedic rituals and was quite willing to patronize cults like Buddhism and Jainism (Kosambi 2008: 108–09,127–30).

Chapter XII

1 Although it is untenable to claim that all Hindus are either Vaishnavites or Saivites, the reverence and worship of Vishnu and Shiva is undoubtedly widespread throughout the subcontinent. This can be attributed to the Puranas which were composed from the beginning of the fourth century CE. Their authors are said to have appropriated folktales and popular beliefs from local storytellers to construct myths with a uniform cast of protagonists: Brahma, Vishnu, Shiva and Devi. Needless to say, of these Vishnu and Shiva were most popular (Doniger 2015: 231–78). The rise of bhakti among the non-Brahmins as a philosophy, and its appropriation by Brahmin pontiffs like Sankara and Ramanuja, also contributed to this phenomenon. Its focus moved away from ritualism towards devotion to the figure (usually) Vishnu and Shiva, in one form or another (Doniger 2015: 295–304).

2 [The Brahmins of India fall into two divisions (1) Pancha Dravid and (2) Pancha Gauda. The former are vegetarians, the latter are not.] Rosalind O'Hanlon (2013) claims that the concretization of the Pancha Dravida and Pancha Gauda categories is relatively new. The new classification became necessary in the sixteenth and seventeenth centuries, when there was a marked inequality between Brahmins, some of whom were quite poor while others prospered. This necessitated a renewed need to look at what exactly made a Brahmin (and who was superior to whom). Until the early centuries of the second millennium, Brahmins identified themselves through the Vedic shakhas they studied and their gotras. In the medieval

period, Benarasi Brahmins sought to classify all Brahmins within ten large groupings, five each for Northern and Southern India: Pancha Gaudas and Pancha Dravidas

3 Asoka was the emperor of the Maurya dynasty from 268 to 232 BCE. He was the grandson of Chandragupta Maurya and ruled over the largest empire known to the subcontinent. He famously adopted the Buddhist dhamma and propagated it within and beyond South Asia. Just like Buddhism came under siege on Indian soil from a resurgent Brahmanism, the memory of Asoka was also erased. He stepped out of the mists of history owing to the work of European archaeologists and philologists as outlined by Charles Allen in *Ashoka: The Search for India's Lost Emperor* (2012). Among the primary sources on Asoka are the Pillar and Rock Edicts erected by him.

4 The Rock Edict No. I was found inscribed onto a boulder in Girnar near Junagadh, Gujarat. It covers about a hundred square-feet area, rising to twelve feet in height and with a circumference of seventy-five feet (Hultzsch 1925: ix–x).

5 The second and fifth pillar edicts Ambedkar refers to here are found on the Delhi-Topra pillar, which is one among the six pillars discovered with Asokan edicts. Made of pink sandstone and forty-two feet and seven inches in length, the Delhi-Topra pillar contains seven edicts. It originally stood in the village of Topra (in present-day Haryana) and was moved to Delhi by Sultan Firoz Shah (1351–88 CE) of the Tughlaq dynasty (Hultzsch 1925: xv–xvi).

6 The following reference is taken from Vincent Smith's *Asoka—The Buddhist Emperor of India* (1909), pages 155–56. Smith (1848–1920) was a British Indologist and art historian at Oxford, who had worked as an administrator in the then United Provinces, India.

7 Taken from Smith 1909: 183–84, under the heading "The Royal Example". Inconsistencies in Ambedkar's extract have been fixed here.

8 Smith 1909: 186–89. The title under which Pillar Edict No. V occurs

in Smith's rendition is: "Regulations restricting slaughter and mutilation of animals".

9 Emphasis added by Ambedkar.

10 Emphasis added by Ambedkar.

11 Tishya and Punarvasu are lunar constellations; the day of the full moon for the particular constellation is considered auspicious. The scholar Nayanjot Lahiri writes, 'Possibly, Tishya signified Asoka's birth-star and Punarvasu his anointment' (2015: 274).

12 In the *Manusmriti* it is established that 'those that do not move are food for those that move, and those that have no fangs are food for those with fangs; those that have no hands are food for those with hands; and cowards are the food of the brave' (5.29; Doniger and Smith 1991: 110). While the cow is the most revered animal in the text, there is no injunction against its slaughter. Only the caveat that the consumption of meat must be treated as, and preceded by, a 'sacrifice'.

13 The extract is taken from Georg Bühler's translation of the *Manusmriti* (1886: 171–72).

14 [Smith – *Asoka*, p. 58] The quote is from Vincent Smith's *Asoka: The Buddhist Emperor of India* (1909). Although Smith concedes that Jains and Brahmanical Hindus conform to the same notion of sanctity of (animal) life, he also says that early Hinduism did not have similar values and that sacrificial killing of animals was an important part of their sacred rituals. He states that the origin of present-day reverence Hindus hold for cows was 'very curious [and] imperfectly solved' (Smith 1909: 58).

15 [Mookerji, *Asoka*, p. 21, 182, 184] Radhakumud Mookerji (1884–1964), a practitioner of nationalist historiography, states in his book *Asoka* that: '[Asoka's proclamation prohibited] the slaughter of numerous birds and beasts specified besides "all four-footed animals which are neither utilised nor eaten," such as the cow, for example, which was never used as a pack-animal nor for food in India' (Mookerji 1928: 21). Further: 'But a similar inference from the omission of the cow in the list, as made by

V. A. Smith, is untenable, because the cow had been protected by popular religious opinion long before Asoka, and would also come under the class of quadrupeds which are 'not eaten' (khadiyati)' (1928: 182).

16 Gabriel Tarde (1843–1894) was a French sociologist, criminologist and social psychologist who significantly contributed to 'social interaction theory and to diffusion research' (Kinnunen 1996: 431). He developed a theory of how imitation led to the spread of beliefs and practices in society. Ambedkar often made references to Tarde's theories, most notably in his 1916 paper, "Castes in India: Their Mechanism, Genesis and Development."

17 It has not been possible to establish the existence or provenance of such a Purana.

Chapter XIII

1 Ambedkar also refers to this phenomenon as a 'counterrevolution' in his posthumously published manuscript "Revolution and Counter-Revolution in Ancient India" (Ambedkar 1987). The book presents a close reading of the influential Hindu text, Bhagavad Gita. Launching an attack on the Gita's idea of morality, Ambedkar shows exactly how it was a counter-revolutionary text which was produced in the wake of the true revolutionary break in society which came from Buddhism.

2 The *Aitareya Brahmana* is linked to the Rig Veda and it acts as a manual of duties and explanation for the seven Hotri priests: Hotar, Maitravaruna (Prasastar), Brahmanachhamsi, Achhavaka, Potar, Nestar and Agnidhra. In particular, the Brahmana details how to carry out sacrifices which include those to Agni and Soma, the relation of the Hotri priests with the Kshatriyas, and the distribution of meat after the performance of a sacrifice (Haug 1922: xl–xlviii).

3 The Yupa symbolizes death and killing and is closely associated with the Vedic weapon vajra—the lightning bolt sword wielded by Indra. When Indra smote Vrtra, the serpent/dragon Asura who symbolized drought, the vajra is said to have been sundered into four forms: a wooden sword (sphya)

which is used to demarcate the area within which sacrifices are conducted, a Yupa, a chariot, and arrows (Hiltebeitel 1991). According to the *Aitareya Brahmana*, the Yupa was the means by which the gods debarred humans from entering the celestial world. It was erected at the spot where the gods themselves had performed sacrifices to enter the sacred realm. Upon finding the Yupa, men and rishis dug it out, and turned it upside down to point it heavenwards. The sacred sacrifices were thus revealed to them and the celestial world was made known, equalizing the Brahmins with the gods (Haug 1863: 72–73).

4 [*Aitareya Brahmana* II, p. 72–74] The quotes from the *Aitareya Brahmana* that follow are taken from Martin Haug's 1863 translation.

5 [*Aitareya Brahmana* (Martin Haug) II, p. 74–78.]

6 The Hotar is a Brahmin priest who specializes in the study and recitation of the Rig Veda. Hotar can also be translated as 'pourer (of ghee)' (Jamison and Witzel 1992: 35–37). Hermann Oldenberg (1993: 214) also contends that the Hotar corresponds with the old-Iranian Avestic Zaotar, who was the reciter of Gathas in Iranian Soma-sacrifices.

7 A description of the animal to be sacrificed is also given: 'They say: the animal to be offered to Agni–Soma must be of two colours, because it belongs to two deities. But this (precept) is not to be attended to. A fat animal is to be sacrificed; because animals are of a fat complexion, and the sacrifice (if compared with them) certainly lean. When the animal is fat, the sacrifice thrives through its marrow' (Haug 1863: 80). The text also urges the disciples to disregard any injunctions to abstain from meat-eating and to follow the example of Indra.

8 [*Aitareya Brahmana* (Martin Haug) II, p. 84–86.]

9 The Adhvaryu is the sacrificial priest who tends the fire and performs the physical actions necessary for the ritual, while the Hotar recites the mantras. He is the chief guardian of the fire and the straw and is responsible for the purification of the tools used.

10 [*Aitareya Brahmana* (Martin Haug) II, p. 86.]

11 Sathaye (1969) claims that according to the *Aitareya Brahmana* it is the Brahman (and not the lower order priests: Hotar, Adhvaryu, etc.) who gets the largest and choicest portions of the sacrificed animal.

12 [As a matter of fact the Brahmins took the whole carcass. Only one leg each was given to the sacrificer and his wife.]

13 [*Aitareya Brahmana* (Martin Haug) II, p. 86–87.]

14 [*Aitareya Brahmana* (Martin Haug) II, p. 86-90]

15 The word 'Adhrigu' has been variously interpreted by scholars as: 'one who possesses cows shut in a mountain stronghold', 'one who does not go disgruntled', 'one whose cow is generous and doesn't hold her milk', 'one who is not poor', 'possessor of castrated bulls, and therefore wealthy'. Several scholars also attest to its Avestan origins. In Vedic literature the usage of Adhrigu is limited to the Rig Veda, and it is likely that authors of the later texts were not privy to the meaning of the word. Apart from referring to obscure individuals the word also describes the following gods: Indra, Agni, the Maruts, the Asvins, and Soma; notably the Adityas, Mitra or Varuna are not associated with it (Thompson 2002).

16 Though the Sanskrit term 'apapa' may refer to sinless or virtuous, Haug points out the play on words here: 'apa' also means 'Away!' and in the mantra its repetition is used to signify the name of the slaughterer (Haug 1863: 89n18).

17 Japa is the practice of repetitive chanting of a god's name. It is usually performed with rosary beads.

18 [*Aitareya Brahmana* (Martin Haug) II, p. 87.]

19 There are two kinds of sacrifices in Vedic literature: haviryajna and soma. The difference lies in the kinds of rites that are performed. In a harivyajna animal sacrifice (pasubandha), for instance, the Brahmin offers the sacrificer a part of the food according to rituals, and leads him to stride in water that has been poured out by the priest. The soma sacrifice does not contain these rites. The soma rite is performed (as is obvious) with soma,

while haviryajna is a sacrifice of milk (Thite 1970; Lidova 1994).

20 [*Aitareya Brahmana* (Martin Haug) II, p. 93.]

21 [Manota means the deity to whom the offering is dedicated.]

22 [*Aitareya Brahmana* (Martin Haug) II, p. 441–42.]

23 Although the Rig Veda does not have a rhyming scheme, each section is written in a specific metre. Each stanza has a fixed number of quarter verses (pada), generally three or four, and each pada has a fixed number of syllables. Usually padas in a stanza are of equal length and conform to a particular metre, but on occasion a single stanza can contain two or more kinds of metres. The Brihati metre consists of four padas and a total of thirty-six syllables. The first, second and fourth line contain eight syllables each and the third line contains twelve syllables (Griffith 1896; Haug 1863).

24 Devabhaga is one of the brothers of Vasudeva, father of Krishna in the Mahabharata.

25 The *Aitareya Brahmana* tries to explain away the fact that it was the human who was at the centre at this ritualistic sacrifice. In a section which follows the rituals listed by Ambedkar, it is explicitly mentioned that the gods demanded human sacrifice. However, the 'part' of man which was fit for sacrifice leaves him and enters a series of animals.

26 [*Aitareya Brahmana* (Martin Haug) II, p. 80.]

27 The following extracts have been taken from Georg Bühler's translation, *The Laws of Manu* (1886: 173–77), all from Chapter V, entitled "Lawful and Forbidden Food".

28 Prajapati, in Vedic literature, refers to the creator of the universe. There are several accounts of the creation myth. The most important one is the "Purusha Sukta" of the Rig Veda, in which Prajapati is described as the primordial man (purusha) who is sacrificed, and from whose parts the world arises. In later Hinduism 'Prajapati' was a moniker for Brahma (Lochtefeld 2002). The *Puranic Encyclopaedia* entry under this head claims: 'Creators of the world. With a view to making creation easy Brahma at first created

twenty-one Prajapatis (creators). They are Brahma, Rudra, Manu, Daksa, Bhrgu, Dharma, Tapa, Yama, Marici, Angiras, Atri, Pulastya, Pulaha, Kratu, Vasistha, Paramesthi, Surya, Candra, Kardama, Krodha and Vikrita' (Mani 1975).

29 One who has undergone the ritual samavartana, the rite that 'bathes one in knowledge', is known as a Snataka. The samavartana marks the end of studenthood and a return to household. In direct contrast to the upanayana rites which are ascetic in nature, the samavartana thrusts the individual into domestic life (Toomey 1976: 40–45).

30 [Manu, 209] Ambedkar here mistakenly gives us the section number rather than the page number. The exact verse is IV.209 (Bühler 1886: 161). All nine prohibitions that follow are not exact quotes, but paraphrases.

31 [Ibid., 38] Verse IV.38 (Bühler 1886: 135).

32 [Ibid., 45] Verse IV.45 (Bühler 1886: 136).

33 [Ibid., 48] Verse IV.48 (Bühler 1886: 136).

34 [Ibid., 58] Verse IV.58 (Bühler 1886: 138).

35 [Ibid., 59] Verse IV.59 (Bühler 1886: 138).

36 [Ibid., 70] Ambedkar points to the wrong verse here. It is verse IV.72 (Bühler 1886: 140).

37 [Ibid., 162] Verse IV.162 (Bühler 1886: 154).

38 [Ibid., 142] Verse IV.142 (Bühler 1886: 151).

39 On reading the original texts which Ambedkar paraphrases in the above guidelines for the Snataka, it is clear that the conclusion he draws here, that the cow was considered impure, is a bit of a stretch. By this logic even water, fire and fellow Brahmins would have to be considered impure by a Snataka. At most, it can be said that the current understanding of 'purity' and 'impurity' could not be applied to the cow during the time of the conception of *Manusmriti*. Further, it seems unnecessary for Ambedkar to establish that cows were considered impure by Manu; the other evidence

he gathers here points to the reactionary and uneasy relationship of Brahmanism with cows.

40 Ambedkar here renders the end of the extract (Bühler 1886: 75) as, 'present of a cow (the honey-mixture)', whereas in the original it is given as, 'with (the present of) a cow (and the honey-mixture).' In the Doniger and Smith translation (1991: 43) the verse is given as: 'When he is recognized as one who has, by fulfilling his own duties, received the legacy of the Veda from his father, he should first be seated on a couch, adorned with garlands, and honoured with (an offering made from the milk of) a cow.'

41 From Bühler 1886: 172.

42 In Vedic Hinduism, mortal sins are known as a Mahapataka, whereas minor sins are called Upapataka. Sin is inextricably tied with the concept of dharma in Hinduism, which are not a set of generalizable rules (Dhand 2002), but rather codes of conduct inextricably tied to caste and gender.

43 From Bühler 1886: 441.

44 Ambedkar slightly alters the verse here. In the Bühler original it reads: 'Slaying kine, sacrificing for those who are unworthy to sacrifice, adultery, selling oneself, casting off one's teacher, mother, father, or son, giving up the (daily) study of the Veda, and neglecting the (sacred domestic) fire' (Bühler 1886: 442).

45 Manu also offers penances suitable for minor sins which cause the loss of caste in the verses IX.109–11 (Bühler 1886: 453–54).

46 [Yaj. III. 227 and III 234.] It is unclear what in the *Yajnavalkya Smriti* Ambedkar is referring to here. The cited chapter (Chapter III) mostly deals with guidelines pertaining to wedding rituals, with minimal references to the cow. But there are references to the cow in other chapters: Chapter V tells us that those who 'unlawfully' slay beasts will endure a horrible hell (Vidyarnava 1918: 274); Chapter V lists 'lawful' examples of meat consumption (Vidyarnava 1918: 229).

47 The *Vedanta Sutra* (or the *Brahma Sutra*), along with the Upanishads

and Bhagavad Gita, is considered a canonical text of the Vedanta school of philosophy. The *Vedanta Sutra*, attributed to Badarayana, was written around 200 CE, to counter the dualistic interpretations of the Upanishads, promulgated by such Sankhya philosophers. It was also opposed to the adherence to and reduction of religion to the ritualistic pronouncements of the Brahmanas by such schools as the Purva Mimamsa. The *Vedanta Sutra* was born out of the necessity for systematizing contradictory views and philosophies that rose because of varying ritualistic interpretations of the Vedas and the contradictions inherent in the Vedas themselves

48 The section Ambedkar refers to here (II.1.28) does not explicitly deal with sacrifices. Rather it is an explication of how multiplicity can exist if we proclaim that the universe is one Substance. However, the verse I.1.4 tells us that descriptions of the Brahman (the universal singularity) cannot be found in those passages of the Veda which tell us about direct experiences of agents in the world, which include sacrifices. Juxtaposing this against the passage Ambedkar picks out, it can be argued that the *Vedanta Sutra* grants worldly actions their independence, and acts such as sacrifices which were demanded by the Vedas have no bearing on human existence as part of the Brahman.

49 [Kane's *Dharmasastras* II. Part II. p. 776] Kane, like Ambedkar, points to the strangeness of the fact that from being a commonplace thing cow-slaughter completely vanished from Brahmanical ideology after a time. He states: 'It appears that the causes that led on to the giving up of flesh at least by some people were many, the foremost being the metaphysical conception that one Supreme Entity pervades the whole universe, that all life was one, and that even the meanest insect was a manifestation of the divine Essence and that philosophical truths would not dawn upon the man who was not restrained, free from crude appetites and had not universal kindliness and sympathy' (Kane 1941b: 775–76). This is the section Ambedkar refers to above.

50 The transmigration of the soul or metempsychosis is a thematic found within a variety of religious and spiritual traditions. In Vedic discourse—both

philosophical and spiritual—time functions cyclically, and it is governed by samsara, karma and moksha. It is believed that upon the death of a being, its soul does not cease to exist, but is transferred after an appropriate time to another entity. This is called samsara, and karma, the doings and experiences of one's life, is said to define the station—either low or high—of the next birth. Moksha is the liberation from this eternal cycle of death and rebirth.

51 The *Brahadaranyaka Upanishad*, written in prose, is considered the oldest of the Upanishads. This is supported by at least four pieces of evidence: its length, its lack of organization, its archaic language, and its relationship to earlier Vedic texts. Its very name (literally, 'great forest book') points to a transition from the Aranyaka ('forest books') literature, which followed Brahmana literature. This Upanishad is the first to address many of the questions raised in later texts and is therefore an important source for the development of the tradition. See Olivelle 1999.

52 In VI.2, the connectedness of all existence in its different forms is described using the metaphor of a sacrificial fire. It is revealed how in being cyclical all of life is connected. However only those who possess the knowledge of this cycle and therefore truly worship with faith, are freed from the cycle and can reside in Brahma forever. In addition, those who perform 'sacrificial offering, charity, and austerity conquer the worlds' can also be liberated (Hume 1921: 163).

53 Uma Chakravarti (1987) argues that the Buddha's sangha had a heterodox representation as far as caste was concerned, and the hierarchy of the bhikkus that comprised it was set along the lines of seniority. This experimental organization provided an alternative to existing structures in society. Chakravarti argues that the Buddhist conception of kula (divided along the lines of Brahamanas, Khattiyas and Gahapatis) poses a challenge to the Brahmanical four-varna order. In the Buddhist schema, the Khattiyas were considered superior to the Brahmanas. However, the question remains if it sought to undo the concept of birth-based hierarchy as such.

54 Gail Omvedt's survey of the ancient subcontinental landscape finds that Buddhism was deeply rooted in the imperial traditions that emerged

in the first millennium CE, and even earlier. In the kingdoms of Kosala and Magadha, the rulers Pasenadi, Bimbisara and Ajatasattu were all Buddhist 'sympathizers'. The 'Buddhist viharas, stupas, caves including chaitya halls and monasteries, statues' all predated the Brahmanic temples, which only first emerged in the time of the Guptas, the third century CE onwards (Omvedt 2003: 118–19).

55 According to Robert DeCaroli (2004), this adoption of image worship in Buddhism was a direct result of the loss of royal patronage which resulted in its having to ingratiate itself with a multiplicity of religious practices which did not fall within the pale of Brahmanism. This is surmised from archaeological remains of statues of spirit-deities: 'the visual and textual evidence for most types of spirit-deity worship points to a widespread set of practices that centered on images or altars (benches, thrones, etc.) set in fenced enclosures to which people turned in times of need or to mark important transitions (such as the birth of a child)' (DeCaroli 2004: 68). The influence of these diverse practices on present-day Hinduism is palpable: 'the wide-eyed gazes seen on all the images [of spirit-deity sculptures provided by DeCaroli] may suggest a link to modern Hindu *darsan* (ritually seeing and being seen by the deity), which would further confirm their function as objects of ritual devotion' (63).

56 Wendy Doniger (2010) claims that the first substantial cluster of Hindu temples were built around the sixth century CE under the rule of the Pallavas in Southern India (2010: 345).

57 Kancha Ilaiah elaborates on this point in *God as Political Philosopher: Buddha's Challenge to Brahminism* (2001) arguing that the mindless need to offer cattle to yajnas came to be slowly opposed by the Sudra and Vaishya communities that not only were influenced by the Buddha but also had an agricultural and economic interest in saving cattle.

58 Ilaiah likewise argues that the Buddha's doctrine of limited non-violence and opposition to killing cattle converted the Brahmanical forces to vegetarianism and the Buddha was eventually inducted as one of the avataras of Vishnu (2001: 224).

59 Yuan Chwang, alternatively known as Hsuan Tsang and Xuanzang, was a Buddhist monk who travelled from China to India in the seventh century CE. In his sixteen years of travel across the subcontinent, he recorded descriptions of the interaction between the separate forms of Buddhism practised in India and China (Watters 1904).

60 Thomas Watters (1840–1901), served in many administrative positions in British China, and produced English translations of Hsuan Tsang, Lao Tzu, Confucius and several other ancient Chinese authors and texts.

61 Yuan Chwang (1904) Vol. I p. 55] Thomas Watters' *On Yuan Chwang's Travels in India 629–645* was edited by T.W. Rhys Davids and S.W. Bushell and was only published after his passing in 1904.

62 Vaisali was the capital city of the Vajji Confederacy of Mithila, one of the sixteen Mahajanapadas of the ancient Indian subcontinent (in the sixth to fourth centuries BCE). It is an important location in Jain and Buddhist traditions.

63 The *Ssu-fen-lu* or the *Shi-bun-ritsu* is a translation of the *Dharmagupta Vinaya* by Buddhayasas, a Sramana from present-day Kabul, and Choh-fo-nien in 405 CE. It was a central Vinaya text studied in China and Japan, and it gained prominence through its adoption by the Kai Ritsu school established by Dosen Risshi in eighth-century Japan (Petzold 1995). Vinayas are rulebooks based on the Buddha's teachings which are meant to be guides to live an ethical Buddhist life.

64 Doniger and Smith write in their introduction to *The Laws of Manu* (1991): 'Vegetarianism was far more than an interesting new dietary custom. It was a focal point for what might be called a revaluation of all values in ancient India ... at about the same time as the composition of Manu, the full extent of the reversal of Vedic ideals is striking' (xxxiii).

65 Smith (1909) writes: 'It is noteworthy that Asoka's rules do not forbid the slaughter of cows, which, apparently, continued to be lawful. The problem of the origin of the intense feeling of reverence for the cow, now

felt by all Hindus, is a very curious one and still unsolved' (58).

66 Mahapataka denotes the Four Great Crimes in the Vedic tradition. They are: murdering a Brahmin (brahmahatya), stealing a Brahmin's gold (steya), drinking liquor (surapana), or committing adultery with the wife of one's guru (gurutalpaga) (Klostermaier 2007: 141–42).

67 The Guptas were the imperial family of the Gupta dynasty, which ruled a large portion of the subcontinent from 240 CE to 590 CE. Spread over the Indo-Gangetic basin, their imperium is associated with a revival of Hinduism (Kosambi 2008: 192–98).

68 [*Some Aspects of Ancient Indian Culture* (1940), p. 78–79] D.R. Bhandarkar (1875–1950) was an epigraphist and archaeologist. He was the son of the pioneering Indologist Ramchandra Gopal Bhandarkar.

69 An arhant is a person who has achieved enlightenment. It also describes the highest stage of enlightenment in Mahayana Buddhism and is often used as by-word for the Buddha himself; several schools, however, separate an arhant from the Buddha (Warder 2004: 314).

Chapter XIV

1 [This definition of religion is by Prof Emile Durkheim. See his *The Elementary Forms of the Religious Life*, p. 47. For the discussion that follows I have drawn upon the same authority.] Emile Durkheim (1858–1917), one of the founders of sociology, established the discipline as an objective study of society, much like the natural sciences. In his last work, *The Elementary Forms of the Religious Life* (1912/1995), he gives a functionalist definition of religion, where religious belief and practices are in effect the bonds which hold society together.

2 [Prof Durkheim's *The Elementary Forms of the Religious Life*, p. 38] See Durkheim 1912/1995: 38.

3 In his introduction to *The Sacred in a Secular Age: Toward Revision in the Scientific Study of Religion* (1985), Philip E. Hammond draws out

the difference between the religious and the sacred. Building on Georg Simmel's ideas, he suggests that the sacred need not always be tied with the religious, especially in the (purportedly) secular age in which we now find ourselves. 'Encounter with the sacred, or what Simmel calls "piety", is thus not necessarily religion, but "religion in a quasi-fluid state..." (1954: 24), that is, not yet "objectified"' (1985: 3). This state of piety, or the distinction between the sacred and the profane, Hammond writes, is seen by Durkheim and Simmel not as intrinsic to humanity, but a necessary outcome of social organization.

4 [The curious may refer to page 317 of the above book.] This section describes Durkheim's position on the origin of religion in 'collective effervescence': People living in the simplest societies experienced this effervescence when they gathered for collective acts such as harvests. When engaged in collective action people became aware of something larger than themselves, which they interpreted as belonging to the spiritual realm.

5 [*The Elementary Forms of the Religious Life*, p 41. Interdictions which come from religion must be distinguished from those which proceed from magic. For a discussion of this subject see ibid., 300.] According to Durkheim, religious interdictions are concerned with categorizing sacrilegious activities. Magical interdictions, however, have a secular structure and follow a certain reasoned discourse. Breaking such taboos do not offend opinion but rather have consequences that naturally follow from the actions.

6 Durkheim goes to some length about the interdictions made by religion (1915: 300–08). On the subject of food, he draws out two categories: food forbidden to the profane on account of its sacredness and food forbidden to the sacred on account of its profanity.

7 The concept of categorical imperatives lies at the centre of Kantian ethics. It was developed by Immanuel Kant in *Groundwork in The Metaphysics of Morals* (1785). For Kant, moral duties were categorical imperatives, i.e., that which we have to follow unconditionally even though we have the freedom to not do so.

8 The terms 'association' and 'associated life' have a special significance for Ambedkar. He borrows it from Deweyan philosophy, wherein democracy is seen not merely as a political tool, but an essential aspect of social life in all its quarters: education, personal relationships and so on.

9 Mahar is an Untouchable caste in western India that was forced to offer baluta or compulsory service to the caste Hindus of the village. For this, Mahars received not wages but a share in the village produce. Disposing of dead cattle (finding a use for everything 'from the tip of the horn to the end of the tail', as Daya Pawar notes in *Baluta* [2015]), the privilege of skinning cows, guarding the village perimeter, announcing the births and deaths in Savarna households that held them vassal—fifty-two such impositions that passed for rights. Under the colonial government, several Mahars found employment as soldiers in British regiments. Ambedkar himself was the son of a subedar in the British Indian Army. (For an account of the 'Mahar army tradition' to which Ambedkar belonged, see Zelliot [2013: 45–52].)

10 Untouchables were traditionally not allowed to join martial ranks. However, under the Muslim rulers of the second millennium several 'outcastes' were recruited as soldiers and they grew to be quite influential. One such soldier was Amritnak, in the employ of the king of Bedar. He managed to convince the king to pass a 'Charter of 52 Rights' for the Mahars. These included the right to collect baluta, a small sum in lieu of the services that the Mahars provided in the villages. This, R.K. Kshirsagar notes, proved to be detrimental to the Mahars: even though they now had a few petty rights, it was expected of them to carry out all the 'dirty' and hazardous tasks. Their conditions worsened under the rule of the Brahmin peshwas who imposed severe restrictions on them and intensified their degradation (Kshirsagar 1994).

11 The zeal for cow-protection was only one of the ways in which Brahmanism was revived under the Guptas. Rejecting the homegrown art, created by those of the lower social order, which flourished under Buddhist influence, they embraced the Hellenist-inspired Gandhara style. Several attempts to rewrite old religious texts were also undertaken. These

would include Kalidasa's expansive rendering of Shakuntala's story from the Mahabharata and also the rewriting of the Bhagavad Gita. Reinterpretations of the multifarious Puranas and the writing of Dharmasastras were undertaken. With the reach of the empire being so wide, several non-Brahmin mendicants tried to become chroniclers and bards to sneak in their own ideas into the Brahmanical fold. This was allowed, but attempts were also made to 'Puranicize' the plural ideas and make them palatable to the conservative tastes of the ruling ideology. The cult of Vaishnavism also became the phenomenon that it is, thanks to the patronage of the Gupta kings (Doniger 2010).

12 Imitation was an important concept which Ambedkar deployed in his 1916 paper delivered in New York City, "Castes in India: Their Genesis, Mechanism and Development", in which he tried to map the conceptual logic of the emergence of caste. He borrowed the concept from the theories of Walter Bagehot and Gabriel Tarde.

13 [Owing to the reform movement among the Mahars the position has become just the reverse. The Mahars refuse to take the dead animal while the Hindu villagers force them to take it.]

Chapter XV

1 Current scholarship affirms Ambedkar's. Olivelle (1999: xxiv) says that a large number of works dealing with dharma—written in an aphoristic style known as Sutra—were likely composed in the centuries immediately prior to the common era, and that they 'belong to the same literary tradition that produced the works comprising the scriptural corpus of the Veda' (xxv). Most Dharma Sutras are lost and only four—of Apastamba, Gautama, Vasishtha and Baudhayana—have survived.

2 Ambedkar's secondary source for the table reproduced here is Kane's chapter on "Untouchability" in *History of Dharmasastras (Ancient and Medieval Religious and Civil Law) Vol. II, Part I* that details references to ideas of Untouchables/Untouchability since the Rigvedic period.

3 The *Apastamba Dharma Sutra* has only two books. Kane lists III.1 as featuring the term Antya and following him Ambedkar lists the same, but Olivelle's edition of the four major Dharma Sutras including Apastamba does not feature a Book 3.

4 Ambedkar lists this vide Kane 1941: 70. There are no scholarly editions of *Atri Smriti* or *Likhita Smriti* that could be referred to. Atri is a Rigvedic ancestor; Mandala V of the Rig Veda is attributed to him and known as the Atri Mandala, though Jamison and Brereton say he was not the author of all the verses in the Mandala but his gotra-clan, the Atris, sang most of them (2014: 659). The *Atri Smriti* takes his antiquated name merely as a legitimacy-seeking exercise, just like many shastraic texts claim mythic rishis as authors.

5 Both Ambedkar (1948: 132) and the BAWS edition list this erroneously as '1.2.39.18' via his source Kane (1941: 70) who lists it as '1.3.9.18'.

6 This seems to be an error since the required details of Manu are not given; also Kane (1941: 70) does not list Manu as one of the sources of Bahya; the references to *Vishnu Dharma Sutra* and *Narada Smriti* that follow via Kane do tally.

7 Kane gives this as 155, and in Ambedkar (1948: 132) and BAWS (1990a) it is I.155; however, nothing tallies with the first-ever English translation of *Narada Smriti* by Julius Jolly (1876); the use of *Bahya* could not be established in the entire text though the term 'outcast' occurs in five instances in Jolly's English.

8 The reference given here for the *Gautama Dharma Sutra* doesn't appear to make sense; it's likely a typo or an oversight. The text of *Gautama Dharma Sutra* is divided into 28 chapters and each chapter is further subdivided into numbered verses. So references would have to be given as '28.4', for example. In Patrick Olivelle's translation, no reference to the term 'Antyavasin' can be found.

9 *Madhyamangiras* appears to be another ghost text cited by Ambedkar and is not listed in Kane's *History of Dhamasastra* (1941). See Jha 1979: 103.

10 It has not been possible to establish this in Mitakshara's commentary even via Kane (1941).

11 It has not (yet) been possible to access a reliable edition of the *Vyasa Smriti* attributed to Vyasa though it is much cited via secondary sources by several scholars from Kane and Ambedkar to D.N. Jha.

12 Mikael Aktor says that despite this proliferation of terms, there was a lack of consensus on what each meant. He tells us that it is possible that all this nomenclature could possibly be a speculative exercise, a means of identifying and creating a 'differentiated inclusion' of indigenous and foreign people in the system of varna (2018: 93). See also Chakravarti 1987: 29; Sharma 1958/1990: 332–45.

13 'Ancient and medieval texts frequently refer to what looks like proto-untouchable groups, such as Candalas, Pulkasas, and Svapacas. But these texts are literary sources in which direct evidence of the actual historical, economic, and social conditions of these groups is very limited. Even the legal literature, the *Dharmasastra*, in which we find the most systematic account of the phenomenon, is not a source for the history of the untouchables but, at most, a source for Brahmanical attitudes that to some extent have been influential in forming the later observed social practices' (Aktor 2002: 244).

14 [See Manu I.45]. Both Ambedkar (1948) and BAWS edition (1990a) cite Manu wrongly. It is Chapter X that discusses 'mixed castes' at length and the matching reference to Dasyus appears in X.45: 'All those tribes in this world, which are excluded from (the community of) those born from the mouth, the arms, the thighs, and the feet (of Brahman), are called Dasyus, whether they speak the language of the Mlekkhas (barbarians) or that of the Aryans' (Bühler 1886: 413).

15 [Ibid.] The use of Bahya, spelt Vâhya in Bühler's text, occurs at X.28: 'As a (Brahmana) begets on (females of) two out of the three (twice-born castes a son similar to) himself, (but inferior) on account of the lower degree (of the mother), and (one equal to himself) on a female of his own race, even so is the order in the case of the excluded (races, vâhya)' (Bühler 1886: 408).

16 Hina as a generic reference to 'low' castes is found in contemporaneous and pre-Mauryan Buddhist texts as well. Many scholars, including Chakravarti (1987, 101) point to how in Buddhist texts, '[a] basic opposition between high and low appears in the context of jati, kula, kamma (work) and sippa (craft); thus there are high jatis and low jatis. ... Thus ukkatta [high] jati is defined as khattiya [Pali for kshatriya] and brahmana, while hina jati is defined as candala, vena, nesada, ratthakara, and pukkusa. The latter categories are conventionally translated as low-caste man, bamboo worker or basket maker, hunter, cartwright, and flower sweeper or scavenger, by Buddhist scholars. The same division is repeated exactly in the same form further on in the Vinaya Pitaka.' Ambedkar, as such, can be faulted for bias and for bypassing Buddhist texts in his surveys and this has been pointed to by scholars such as R.S. Sharma (1958/1990) and Vivekanand Jha (2018).

17 IV.79: 'Let him not stay together with outcasts, nor with Kandalas, nor with Pukkasas, nor with fools, nor with overbearing men, nor with low-caste men, nor with Antyavasayins' (Bühler 1886: 141).

18 Medhatithi's *Manubhashya* is one of the most cited commentaries on the *Manusmriti*. With no biographical facts available about its mysterious author, scholars have speculated that he lived in Kashmir or Nepal. Kane infers from the text that Medhatithi must have lived between 820 CE and before 1050 CE and dates *Manubhashya* to c.900 CE (Kane 1941: xi).

19 Ambedkar is likely citing from Bühler's notes where he summarizes the commentaries of all his predecessors and often offers his own take.

20 On the contrary, Bühler is rather careful in making the distinction between Antya (its attendant suffixes) and low-caste, though often these two terms are used almost interchangeably by commentators. At IV.79 cited above, low-caste men and Antyavasayins are both listed. In fact, by translating less, Bühler allows space for a wide array of jati terms that Manu coins and uses (many of them obsolete and some that may never have existed) instead of resolving the confusion in a language (English) that does not have the vocabulary for so many ways of being unequal.

21 [Kane, *History of Dharmasastras* II. Part I. p. 167.]

22 [Kane, *History of Dharmasastras*. Vol. II. part I. p. 70] In the ensuing paragraph, Ambedkar paraphrases Kane.

23 The reference in Kane pertains to *Saraswativilasa*, a digest on 'ancient Hindu Law' written by Prataprudradeva (1497–1540 CE), a king of the Gajapati dynasty in Orissa. *Saraswativilasa* is considered a part of Dharmasastra commentarial literature (see Ellis 1833; Sastry 1927).

24 Bhillama II was a king of the dynasty known as Seuna or Sevuna Yadavas of Devagiri that ruled the Deccan after starting as feudatories of the Chalukyas. Bhillama II ruled from c. 985–1005 CE (Sen 1988: 403).

25 *Viramitrodaya* is a vyavahara text (a law digest) written in the early seventeenth century by Mitra Misra of the 'Benares School' on the Dharmasastra.

26 [Amarkosh II Kanda Brahmabarga Verse II.] The reference is to *Amarakosha*, also known as *Namalinganushasana*, a Sanskrit lexicon written in metrical poetry in the fourth century CE by Amarasimha. A 1913 edition from Poona by Krishnaji Govind Oka opens with these lines: 'Amarasimha's lexicon, well-known to every Sanskrit student, is the oldest work of the kind now extant. It is of great interest to note that, though the production of a Buddhist, it has been universally accepted as an authority by the Brahmans and the Jainas alike' (1913: 3).

27 Including two previous verses that Ambedkar doesn't cite, the reference reads: "1. They declare that the offspring of a Sudra and of a female of the Brahmana caste becomes a Kandala, 2. (That of a Sudra and) of a female of the Kshatriya caste, a Vaina, 3. (That of a Sudra and) of a female of the Vaishya caste, an Antyavasayin' (Bühler 1882: 94).

28 It is erroneously printed as V.39 in Ambedkar (1948, 137) and BAWS (1990a); the right reference is to verse X.39.

29 [According to all Dharma Sutras and Smritis including *Manusmriti*.]

30 [According to *Veda Vyas Smriti* (1.910)] It has not been possible to

establish the provenance of this reference, but the same is cited in Kane.

31 [According to *Veda Vyas Smriti* (1.910)]

32 [According to Yama quoted in Parasura Madhavya] Parasara Madhaviya (spelt as Parasura Madhavya in Ambedkar 1948: 138; and 1990a: 366) was authored in the thirteenth century by Madhavacarya who cites from the *Yama Smriti*, a text often cited in other commentaries but a reliable edition of which has not been found.

33 [Anusasan Parva (29.17). He is also called Matanga.]

34 Ambedkar is citing from Bühler (1898: 253).

35 See Bühler 1882: 30.

36 See Bühler 1882: 171.

37 Manu V.85 (Bühler 1886: 183); Manu V.131 (192); Manu V.143 (194).

38 In Chapter II, titled "Untouchability among Hindus", which does not appear in this edition to keep it at a manageable length, Ambedkar discusses at length Brahmanic notions of ritual pollution, purity and defilement as defined in the *Manusmriti* and such texts, and compares them to the taboos that exist among 'primitive and ancient peoples'. He concludes that 'defilement as observed by the Primitive Society was of a temporary duration', for 'after the period of defilement was over and after the purificatory ceremonies were performed the defilement vanished and the individual became pure and associable. But the impurity of the 50–60 millions of the Untouchables of India, quite unlike the impurity arising from birth, death, etc., is permanent' (1990a: 266).

Chapter XVI

1 [*Dharmasastras* Vol. II Part I. p. 165]

2 VIII.5 is the longest hymn to the Asvins in the Rig Veda. It has little mythological material and no mention of the exploits of the Asvins. Rather

the hymn is an exhortation to perform sacrifices and a prayer to the gods to fulfil desires of supplicants.

3 In the Rig Veda only one reference to a barber is made. It can be found at X.143.4. The hymn X.143 is dedicated to Agni and it speaks of the dangerous nature of fire. The verse is as follows: 'When you travel to the heights and the depths, snapping, you go in all directions, like an army in greedy pursuit./ When the wind fans your flame, like a barber a beard you shave the ground' (Jamison and Brereton 2014: 1628).

4 Vidalakara or Bidalakara refers to bamboo-workers and basket makers. In the *Vajasaneyi Samhita* and the *Taittiriya Brahmana* they are among the 148 victims listed for human sacrifice (purushamedha). In this sacrifice, the Bidalkaras are dedicated to the pisacas, a class of deities that are in the same class as asuras and raksasas; Vivekanand Jha (1978) surmises that this fact points to the aboriginal origin of the caste. The name for the Bidalkaras becomes 'Vena' in the post-Vedic age, and several references to them as hina jatis (lesser castes) can be found in Pali texts.

5 Buruda is a basket-weaving caste from Maharashtra and Telangana (Russell 1916: 209).

6 In the Atharva Veda, Vasahpalpuli is the word used to refer to a female washer of clothes.

7 Rajaka refers to communities involved in the washing of clothes in Andhra Pradesh, Telangana and Sri Lanka. The caste is also referred to as Vannan, Vannar (in Tamil) and Chakali (Telugu).

8 [Manu X.4] 'The Brahmana, the Kshatriya, and the Vaishya castes (varna) are the twice-born ones, but the fourth, the Sudra, has one birth only; there is no fifth (caste)' (Bühler 1886: 402).

9 The *Narada Smriti* comprises of eighteen laws that concern legal and economic proceedings. In a chapter entitled "Head of Dispute", under the subhead 'Breach of Promised Obedience' one can find discussions on existent slavery. Five kinds of labourers are listed, of which four are proclaimed to be free (a pupil, an apprentice, a hired servant and an agent)

and they can be of any caste. The fifth kind, the slave, is said to be of fifteen further types and they are all declared as impure. The jobs assigned to them are: 'Clearing the house, the gateway, the convenience, and the road from rubbish, rubbing the secret limbs, and gathering and removing impurities, especially urine and faeces' (Jolly 1876: 61–62).

10 [Bühler, *Laws of Manu* (S.B.E.) Vol. XXV. Int. CXIVI.] In the mentioned source, Bühler tries to fix the date of *Manusmriti*'s authorship. The difficulty of fixing such a date is discussed at length by Bühler. In their introduction to *The Laws of Manu* (1991), Doniger and Smith also date the text to around the second century CE (xvii).

11 Chander Kishan Daphtary was an Indian lawyer and bureaucrat. He was appointed India's first solicitor general, and was, between 1963 and 1968, the attorney general of India. From 1972 to 1978 he held office in the Rajya Sabha.

12 After the reign of Asoka (269–232 BCE), the Mauryan Empire devolved into a state of instability. This culminated in a revolt carried out by the military general Pushyamitra who assassinated the king Brihadratha and established the Sunga dynasty in 184 BCE. The Sungas are chiefly credited with reviving the Vedic practice of the yajna. Pushyamitra is said to have had strong anti-Buddhist convictions. It is claimed that he destroyed Buddhist monasteries and persecuted monks throughout his empire which stretched from Pataliputra to Sakala. Buddhist texts *Divyavadana* and *Manjusrimulakalpa* ascribe several conflicts to Pushyamitra in which he invaded Buddhist kingdoms, one of which was the conquest of Sakala. They also claim that Pushyamitra died ingloriously while fighting one such battle in the vicinity of his Sakala territory. The Sungas after Pushyamitra were a weak succession of kings, and inroads into their kingdom were made by the Greeks, Satavahanas and tribal chiefs like Kharavela (Kosambi 2008: 187–88).

13 Fa-Hian (CE 399–414), also known as Faxian, was a Buddhist Pilgrim to India. He travelled from China to India, and visited monasteries in what is now Xinjiang, Pakistan, India, Nepal, Bangladesh, and Sri Lanka. Like

Hsuan Tsang, he recorded a survey of 'Buddhistic Kingdoms'.

14 [*Buddhist Records in Western India* by Beal. Introduction p. xxxvii–xxxviii.] The following quote is taken from Samuel Beal's Introduction to his translation of Hsuan Tsang's writings, *Buddhist Records in Western India, Vol. I* (1884). This introduction includes a section which is a translation of Fa-Hian's writings, entitled "The Travels of Fa-Hian: Buddhist Country Records". The above text is part of the sixteenth chapter of Fa-Hian's work, and in another translation, done by James Legge, it is titled as "On to Mathura or Muttra. Condition and customs of Central India; of the monks, viharas, and monasteries". When the term 'Chandala' occurs in Legge's translation for the first time, he provides the following reference from Ernest J. Eitel's Hand *Book of Chinese Buddhism, being A Sanskrit-Chinese Dictionary with Vocabularies of Buddhist Terms*: 'The name Chandalas is explained as "butchers," "wicked men," and those who carry "the awful flag," to warn off their betters;— the lowest and most despised caste of India, members of which, however, when converted, were admitted even into the ranks of priesthood' (Legge 1886: 43).

15 Also known as Banabhatta, Bana was a Brahmin poet and author in the seventh century CE. He was a member of the court of king Harsha of the Vardhana dynasty. Bana is considered one of the greatest Sanskrit writers. His two most famous works are *Harshacharita* and *Kadambari*.

16 *Kadamabari* is considered one of the first novels in world literature. It is a romance that broke the tyranny of fixed metres and is set in free verse. The love story between the main characters, a princess named Kadambari and a prince named Chandripida, is but one element of the book's complex plot. *Kadambari* was left unfinished at Bana's death and is said to have been completed by his son Bhusanabhatta (Sharma 1968).

17 [*Kadambari* (Ridding's Translation), p. 204] Ambedkar is citing from *The Kadambari of Bana* translated by C.M. Ridding and published in 1896 by the Royal Asiatic Society.

18 There are many Matangas, at least four, in Vedic mythology and Puranic

lore. One of them becomes a knowledgeable sage by his deeds despite his low place in the Varna hierarchy and figures in the Buddhist tradition as well. Gail Omvedt shows how in the *Sutta Nipata*, Matanga, the son of a Chandala is eulogised as an example of virtue (2003: 77). She also discusses another real (not mythical) Kasyapa Matanga, a Buddhist missionary who 'left for China in 65 CE' through the treacherous Karakoram route, whose name owes to the 'semi-legendary Candala hero Matanga' (123–24). Omvedt says this might even be the earliest reference to a Dalit in Indian literature. See also Kosambi 1985: 160.

19 [Ibid., p. 8–10] Ambedkar provides a 1,100-word excerpt from *Kadambari* where Bana, in his own narrative voice and in that of the emperor's, describes the celestial beauty of the Chandala maiden in epic terms. We have retained only the key passages here, but the curious may consult BAWS 7 (1990b, 376–77) to read it in full. Given the nature of Kadambari's florid prose-poetry, there's a great deal of fictive excess and exaggeration in describing everything.

20 Ambedkar's comparison of Fa-Hian's non-fictional documentary effort with Bana's fictional, poetic, fantastic excess appears untenable. Besides, Bana's narrative makes it clear that the Chandala woman—who is never named—is an exception and that her birth into such a station is unfortunate.

21 A gotra of the North Indian Saraswat Brahmin caste, it is also known as 'Vatsa' and claims its lineage from the sage Bhrigu (Datta 1989; Somasundaram 1986).

22 [*Kadambari* (Ridding's Translation), p. 204]

23 [Watters-Yuan Chwang Vol. I. p. 147]

References

Aktor, Mikael. 2002. "Rules of untouchability in ancient and medieval law books: Householders, competence, and inauspiciousness". *International Journal of Hindu Studies*, 6(3): 243–74.

———. 2018. "Untouchability." In *Brill's Encyclopedia of Hinduism*. Edited by Knut A. Jacobsen, Helene Basu, Angelika Malinar, Vasudha Narayanan. Consulted online on 22 October 2018.

Allen, Charles. 2012. *Ashoka: The Search for India's Lost Emperor*. London: Abacus.

Alsdorf, Ludwig. 2010. *The History of Vegetarianism and Cow-Veneration in India*. Translated by Bal Patil. Abingdon: Routledge.Ambedkar 1987a

Ambedkar, B.R. 1987. "Revolution and Counter-Revolution" In *BAWS 3*. Edited by Vasant Moon. Bombay: Education Department, Government of Maharashtra. 151–437.

———.1990a. *The Untouchables: Who Were They and Why They Became Untouchables?* In *BAWS 7*. Edited by Vasant Moon. Bombay: Education Department, Government of Maharashtra. 229–382.

———.1990b. *Who Were The Shudras? How they came to be the Fourth Varna in the Indo–Aryan Society*. In *BAWS 7*. Edited by Vasant Moon. Bombay: Education Department, Government of Maharashtra. 1–227.

———. 1990c. *Pakistan or the Partition of India*. In *BAWS 8*. Edited by Vasant Moon. Bombay: Education Department, Government of Maharashtra.

———. 2003. "The Mahars: Who were they and how they became the Untouchables." In *BAWS 17, Part II*. Edited by Hari Narake, M.L. Kasare, N.G. Kamble, Ashok Godghate. Bombay: Education Department, Government of Maharashtra. 137–50.

Bajrange, Dakxin, Sarah Gandee and William Gould. 2018. "Settling the citizen, settling the nomad: 'Habitual offenders', rebellion and civic consciousness in western India, 1938–1952." *White Rose Research*

Online. Cambridge: Cambridge University Press.

Beal, Samuel. 1884. *Si-Yu-Ki: Buddhist Records of the Western World, Translated from the Chinese of Hieun Tsiang, Vol I*. London: Trübner & Co.

Bühler, George. 1882. Trans. *The Sacred Laws of The Aryas: Apastamba, Gautama, Vasishta and Baudhayana. Part 2: Vasishta and Baudhayana.* Oxford: The Clarendon Press.

———. 1886. *The Laws of Manu. Sacred Books of the East 25*. Oxford: Clarendon Press.

———. 1898. Trans. *The Sacred Laws of The Aryas: Apastamba, Gautama, Vasishta and Baudhayana. Part 1: Apastama and Gautama*. New York: The Christian Literature Company.

Carri, Sebastian J. 2000. *Gavesnm: Or, On the Track of the Cow; And, In Search of the Mysterious Word; And, In Search of the Hidden Light.* Wiesbaden: Otto Harrassowitz Verlag.

Chakravarti, Mahadev. 1979. "Beef-Eating in Ancient India." *Social Scientist*, 7(11): 51–55.

Chakravarti, Uma. 1987. *Social Dimensions of Early Buddhism*. New Delhi: Munshiram Manoharlal.

Cotton, J.S. 1911. *Mountstuart Elphinstone, and the Making of Southwestern India*. Oxford: Clarendon Press.

Dalal, Roshen. 2014. *The Vedas: An Introduction to Hinduism's Sacred Texts.* New Delhi: Penguin Books India.

Datta, Swati. 1989. *Migrant Brahmanas in Northern India: Their Settlement and General Impact c. A. D. 475–1030*. Delhi: Motilal Banarsidass Indological Publishers and Booksellers.

DeCaroli, Robert. 2004. *Haunting the Buddha: Indian Popular Religions and the Formation of Buddhism*. New York: Oxford University Press.

Deshpande, Satish and John, Mary E. 2010, June 19. "The Politics of Not Counting Caste". *Economic & Political Weekly*: 39–42.

Devji, Faisal. 2013. *Muslim Zion: Pakistan as a Political Idea*. Massachusetts: Harvard University Press.

Dhand, Arti. 2002. "The Dharma of Ethics, the Ethics of Dharma: Quizzing the Ideals of Hinduism." *The Journal of Religious Ethics*, 30(3): 347–72.

Doniger, Wendy. 2010. *The Hindus: An Alternative History*. Oxford: Oxford University Press.

———. 2015. "Hinduism." In *Norton Anthology of World Religions, Vol. 1*. New York: W.W. Norton & Company, Inc. 53–722.

Doniger, Wendy and Brian K. Smith. 1991. *The Laws of Manu*. London: Penguin Books.

Duncan, Ian. 2005. "Ambedkar, Ambedkarites and the Adivasi: The Dog that Didn't Bark in the Night." Paper delivered at the *International Conference on Reinterpreting Adivasi Movements In South Asia*. Sussex: University of Sussex.

Durkheim, Emile. 1912/1995. *The Elementary Forms of Religious Life*. Translated by Karen E. Fields. New York: The Free Press.

Eggeling, Julius. 1882. *The Satapatha-Brahmana: According to the text of fhe Madhyandina School, Vol. 1. Sacred Books of the East Vol. 12*. Oxford: The Clarendon Press.

———. 1885. *The Satapatha-Brahmana, Vol 2. Sacred Books of the East, Vol. 26*. Oxford: The Clarendon Press.

Ellis, F.W. 1833. "Sources of Hindu Law". *The Law Magazine: Or, Quarterly Review of Jurisprudence*, Vol. 9, Feb–May. London: Saunders and Benning.

Elphinstone, Mountstuart. 1843. *The History of India*. London: John Murray.

Gorky, Maxim. 1982. *On Literature. Collected Works, Volume X*. Moscow: Progress Publishers.

Griffith, Ralph T.B. 1896. *Rig Veda—Book 10*. Benares: E. J. Lazarus and Co.

Hammond, Phillip E. 1985. "Introduction." In *The Sacred in a Secular Age*. Edited by Phillip E. Hammond. Berkeley: University of California Press. 1–6.

Harvey, David Allen. 2012. *The French Enlightenment and its Others: The Mandarin, the Savage, and the Invention of Human Sciences*. New York: Palgrave Macmillan.

Haug, Martin. 1863. *The Aitareya Brahmanam of the Rigveda, Volume 2*. Edited, Translated and Explained by Martin Haug. Bombay: Government Central Book Depot.

———. 1922. *The Aitareya Brahmanam of the Rigveda*. Allahabad: The Panini Office.

Hiltebeitel, Alf. 1991. *The Cult of Draupadi, Volume 2: On Hindu Ritual and the Goddess*. Chicago: The Chicago University Press.

Hultzsch, E. 1925. *Inscriptions of Asoka*. Corpus Inscriptionum Indicarum, Vol. 1. Oxford: Clarendon Press.

Hume, Robert Ernest. 1921. *The Thirteen Principal Upanishads*. London: Oxford University Press.

Ilaiah, Kancha. 2001. *God as Political Philosopher: Buddha's Challenge to Brahminism*. Calcutta: Samya.

Jaffrelot, Christophe. 2002. *Pakistan: Nationalism Without A Nation*. New Delhi: Manohar Publishers and Distributors.

Jamison, S.W. and M. Witzel. 1992. *Vedic Hinduism*. Unpublished Manuscript. https://sites.fas.harvard.edu/~witzel/vedica.pdf.

Jamison, Stephanie and Joel Brereton. 2014. *The Rigveda: The Earliest Religious Poetry of India, Vol. I, 2 and 3*. New York: Oxford University Press.

Jha, D. N. 2009. *The Myth of the Holy Cow*. New Delhi: Navayana.

Jha, Vivekanand. 2018. *Candala: Untouchability and Caste in Early India*. New Delhi: Primus Books.

Jolly, Julius. 1876. *Naradiya Dharmasastra or The Institutes of Narada*. London: Trübner and Co.

Kane, P.V. 1941. *History of Dharmasastras (Ancient and Medieval Religious and Civil Law) Vol II, Part I*. Poona: Bhandarkar Oriental Research Institute.

Keith, Arthur Berriedale. 1920. *Rigveda Brahmanas: The Aitareya and Kausitaki Brahmanas of the Rigveda*. Cambridge: Harvard University Press.

Kinnunen, Jussi. 1996. "Gabriel Tarde as a Founding Father of Innovation Diffusion Research." *Acta Sociologica*, 39(4): 431–42.

Klostermaier, Klaus K. 2007. *A Survey of Hinduism: Third Edition*. Albany:

State University of New York Press.

Kosambi, D.D. 1985. *D.D. Kosambi on History and Society: Problems of Interpretation*. Ed. A.J. Sayed. Bombay: University of Bombay, Dept. of History.

———. 2008. *The Culture and Civilisation of Ancient India in Historical Outline*. Delhi: UBSPD.

Kotani, Hiroyuki. 1997a. "Conflict and Controversy over the Mahar Vatan in the Nineteenth- Twentieth Century Bombay Presidency". In *Caste System, Untouchability and the Depressed.* Edited by H. Kotani. New Delhi: Manohar. 55–78.

——. 1997b. "Ati Südra Castes in the Medieval Deccan". In *Caste System, Untouchability and the Depressed*. Edited by H. Kotani. New Delhi: Manohar. 105–32.

Krishnasamy, K. 2018, May 6. "Devendra Kula Vellalars were wetland farmers, not untouchables, says Krishnasamy." Interviewed by Udhav Nag. *The Hindu*. Accessed 20 November 2018.

Kshirsagar, R.K. 1994. *Dalit Movement in India and Its Leaders, 1857–1956*. New Delhi: MD Publications Pvt Ltd.

Lahiri, Nayanjot. 2015. *Ashoka in Ancient India*. New Delhi: Permanent Black.

Legge, James. 1886. *A Record of Buddhistic Kingdoms; Being an Account by the Chinese Monk Fa-Hien of his Travels in India and Ceylon, A.D. 399–414*. Oxford: Clarendon Press.

Lidova, Natalia. 1994. *Drama and Ritual of Early Hinduism*. Delhi: Motilal Banarsidass Indological Publishers and Booksellers.

Lochtefeld, James G. 2002. *The Illustrated Encyclopaedia of Hinduism*. New York: The Rosen Publishing Group, Inc.

Macnaghten, William Hay. 1860. *Principles of Hindu and Mohammadan Law*. Edited by H. H. Wilson. London: Williams and Norgate.

Mani, Vettam. 1975. *Puranic Encyclopaedia: A Comprehensive Dictionary with Special Reference to the Epic and Puranic Literature*. Delhi: Motilal Banarsidass Indological Publishers and Booksellers.

Mitra, Trailokyanath. 1881. *The Law Relating to the Hindu Widow*.

Calcutta: Thacker, Spinck and Co.
Mookerji, Radhakumud. 1928. *Asoka (Gaekwad Lectures)*. London: MacMillan and Co. Ltd.
O'Hanlon, Rosalind. 2013 . "Contested Conjunctures: Brahman Communities and 'Early Modernity' in India." *The American Historical Review*, 118(3): 765–87.
Ober, Douglas. 2023. *Dust on the Throne: The Search for Buddhism in Modern India*. New Delhi: Navayana.
Oldenberg, Hermann. 1886. *The Grihya-sûtras, rules of Vedic domestic ceremonies*. Translated by Max Müller. Oxford: The Clarendon Press.
———. 1993. *The Religion of the Veda*. Translated by Shridhar B. Shrotri. First published in 1894. Delhi: Motilal Banarsidass Publishers.
Olivelle, Patrick. 1999. *Dharmasutras: The Law Codes of Ancient India*. New York: Oxford University Press.
Olivelle, Patrick and Donald R. Davis, Jr.. Ed. 2018. *The Oxford History of Hinduism Hindu Law: A New History of Dharmasastra*. London: Oxford University Press.
Omvedt, Gail. 2003. *Buddhism in India: Challenging Brahmanism and Caste*. New Delhi: Sage Publications.
Pawar, Daya. 2015. *Baluta*. Translated by Jerry Pinto. New Delhi: Speaking Tiger.
Petzold, Bruno. 1995. *The Classification of Buddhism Bukkyo Kyohan: Comprising The Classification of Buddhist Doctrines in India, China and Japan*. In collaboration with Shinsho Hanayama, edited by Shohei Ichimura. Wiesbaden: Harrassowitz Verlag.
Poliakov, Leon. 2003. *The History of Anti-Semitism, Vol. 3: From Voltaire to Wagner*. Philadelphia: University of Pennsylvania Press.
Rajah, M.C. 1925/2005. *The Oppressed Hindus*. New Delhi: Critical Quest.
Randeria, Shalini. 1989. "Carrion and corpses: conflict in categorizing untouchability in Gujarat". *European Journal of Sociology*, 30(2): 171–91.
Rhys Davids, T.W. 1899. *Dialogues of the Buddha*. Sacred Books of the East, Vol. 11. London: Oxford University Press.

Risley, H.H. and E.A. Gait. 1901. *Census of India, 1901 Volume I: India: Part I—Report*. Calcutta: Government of India Central Printing Office.

Russell, R.V. 1916. *The Tribes and Castes of the Central Provinces of India, Vol II*. London: Macmillan and Co.

Sastry, R. Sharma. 1927. *The Saraswati Vilasa of Prataparudramahadeva Maharaja (Vyavaharakanda)*. Mysore: University of Mysore.

Sathaye, S.G. 1969. "The Aitareya Brahmana and the Republic." *Philosophy East and West*, 19(4): 435–41.

Schwarz, Henry. 2010. *Constructing the Criminal Tribe of Colonial India: Acting Like a Thief*. Oxford: Wiley–Blackwell.

Shank, J.B. 2015. "Voltaire." *The Stanford Encyclopedia of Philosophy*. https://plato.stanford.edu/archives/fall2015/entries/voltaire/. Accessed on 20 November 2018.

Sharma, Neeta. 1968. *Banabhatta: A Literary Study*. Delhi: Munshiram Manoharlal; Oriental Publishers.

Sharma, R.S. 1958/1990. *Sudras in Ancient India*. Delhi: Motilal Banarsidass.

Smith, Vincent A. 1909. *Asoka: The Buddhist Emperor Of India*. Oxford: Clarendon Press.

Solomon, Robert C. 1983. *In the Spirit of Hegel*. New York: Oxford University Press.

Somasundaram, Ottilangam. 1986. "Sexuality in the Kama Sutra of Vatsyayana". *Indian Journal of Psychiatry*, 28(2): 103–08.

Sullivan, Bruce M. 1990. *Krsna Dvaipayana Vyasa and the Mahabharata: A New Interpretation*. Leiden: E. J. Brill.

Sundar, Nandini. 2002. '"Indigenise, nationalise and spiritualise" – an agenda for education?' *International Social Science Journal*, 54(173): 373–83.

Thite, Ganesh Umakant. 1970. "Animal-Sacrifice in the Brahmana texts." *Numen*, 17(2): 143–58.

Thompson, George. 2002. "Adhrigu and drigu: On the Semantics of an Old Indo-Iranian Word." *Journal of the American Oriental Society*, 122(2).

Tikhonov, Nikolay. 1946. "Gorky and Soviet Literature." *The Slavonic and*

East-European Review, 25(64): 28–38.

Toomey, Paul M. 1976. "The Upanayana and Samavartana Rites: A Paradox of Two 'Dharmas.'" *Indian Anthropologist*, 6(1).

Valhe, Vijaya. 2015. "Madhuparka: A Comparative Study (From Agnistomasaptahautraprayoga & Asvalayanagehyasutra)." *Bulletin of the Deccan College Research Institute*, 75.

Varadpande, M. L. 2005. *History of Indian Theatre: Classical Theatre*. New Delhi: Abhinav Publications.

Vidyarnava, Rai Bahadur. 1918. *Yajnavalkya Smriti: with the commentary of Vijnanesvara called The Mitaksara and note from the gloss of Balambhatta*. Allahabad: The Panini Office.

Vishwanath, Rupa. 2014. *The Pariah Problem*. New Delhi: Navayana.

Walshe, Maurice. 1987. *The Long Discourses of the Buddha: A Translation of the Digha Nikaya*. Boston: Wisdom Publications.

Warder, A.K. 2004. *Indian Buddhism*. Delhi: Motilal Banarsidass Publishers.

Watters, Thomas. 1904. *On Yuan Chwang's Yravels in India, 629–645 A.D.* London: Royal Asiatic Society.

Zelliot, Eleanor. 2013. *Ambedkar's World: The Making of Babasaheb and the Dalit Movement*. New Delhi: Navayana.